T0323629

Cambridge Elements

Elements in Defence Economics
edited by
Keith Hartley
University of York

DEFENCE ACQUISITION AND PROCUREMENT

How (Not) to Buy Weapons

Ron P. Smith
Birkbeck, University of London

CAMBRIDGE
UNIVERSITY PRESS

CAMBRIDGE
UNIVERSITY PRESS

University Printing House, Cambridge CB2 8BS, United Kingdom

One Liberty Plaza, 20th Floor, New York, NY 10006, USA

477 Williamstown Road, Port Melbourne, VIC 3207, Australia

314–321, 3rd Floor, Plot 3, Splendor Forum, Jasola District Centre,
New Delhi – 110025, India

103 Penang Road, #05–06/07, Visioncrest Commercial, Singapore 238467

Cambridge University Press is part of the University of Cambridge.

It furthers the University's mission by disseminating knowledge in the pursuit of
education, learning, and research at the highest international levels of excellence.

www.cambridge.org
Information on this title: www.cambridge.org/9781009189651
DOI: 10.1017/9781009189644

First published 2022

A catalogue record for this publication is available from the British Library.

ISBN 978-1-009-18965-1 Paperback
ISSN 2632-332X (online)
ISSN 2632-3311 (print)

Defence Acquisition and Procurement

How (Not) to Buy Weapons

Elements in Defence Economics

DOI: 10.1017/9781009189644
First published online: June 2022

Ron P. Smith
Birkbeck, University of London

Author for correspondence: Ron P. Smith, r.smith@bbk.ac.uk

Abstract: The acquisition and procurement of major weapons systems is fraught with difficulties. They tend to be delivered late, over budget and unable to meet requirements. This Element provides an economic analysis of why this happens. Market structure, demand by the military and supply by the arms firms, shapes the conduct of the agents and generates the poor performance observed. The military are trying to counter an evolving threat, subject to a budget constraint, high R&D costs and new technologies. The interaction between a government made up of warring tribes and arms firms with considerable market and political power is further complicated by a set of what economists call 'principal-agent' problems, which are examined. While the poor performance has prompted many countries to propose reforms, the difficulty of the task and the institutional incentives faced by the actors mean that the reforms rarely solve the problem.

Keywords: acquisition, procurement, weapons systems, principal-agent, defence economics.

JEL classifications: D23, D86, H56, H57, L14, O32

ISBNs: 9781009189651 (PB), 9781009189644 (OC)
ISSNs: 2632-332X (online), 2632-3311 (print)

Contents

1 Introduction

Modern weapons are complex systems, whose purchase is surrounded with difficulties. Their acquisition and procurement involve defence departments making and implementing hard choices, usually given a set of challenging options, in an uncertain environment, with limited information and budget constraints. The uncertainty can be such that when the requirement is specified the technology does not exist; it has to be invented. These difficulties are rarely fully surmounted and as a result new weapons tend to be delivered late, over budget and unable to meet their performance targets. These failures in the acquisition and procurement of most, though not all, systems are repeatedly documented in reports by the US Government Accountability Office (GAO) about the Department of Defense (DOD); the UK National Audit Office (NAO) about the Ministry of Defence (MoD); and government auditors in many other countries about their defence departments, the generic term that will be used when not referring to a specific country. While some other countries will be discussed, the examples will largely be taken from the UK and the USA. The projects discussed include, from the USA, the F-35 Lightning II Joint Strike Fighter and the Future Combat Systems of armoured vehicles; the European A400 M military transport; and, from the UK, the Ajax armoured vehicle, Warrior upgrade and nuclear projects.

Procurement involves buying weapons designed to kill or incapacitate their targets, usually people. The weapons are being used in the many current conflicts around the world. This raises a range of moral and ethical issues. The fact that this Element does not address the moral and ethical issues does not mean that they are unimportant. They are important; it is just that economists have no special expertise in judgements about the moral and ethical dimensions. So this Element will just discuss the issues and leave it to the readers to make their own judgements.

Acquisition and procurement are just one aspect of defence, or defense, economics. Sandler and Hartley (1995) provide a more technical treatment and Smith (2009) a less technical treatment of the wider subject. There is a, probably apocryphal, story that US President Harry Truman asked for a one-armed economist, who could not say 'on the one hand ... on the other hand'. There will be a lot of 'on the one hand ... on the other hand' in this Element; there are no simple answers. The Element examines the economic reasons for the failures in procurement, hence the subtitle 'how (not) to buy weapons', and emphasises the role of incentives and institutional structure. There are books about the engineering and contracting skills needed in military procurement, for instance in the UK *Conquering Complexity* (DEG 2005) and in the USA the

Defense Acquisition Guidebook of the Defense Acquisition University. This is not one of those books. Instead it looks at the economics of the process, broadly following the *structure, conduct, performance* framework, often used in industrial economics. The *structure* of the market, the nature of the demand by the military and the supply by the arms firms, determines their *conduct* in interacting within a fraught contractual relationship, which determines the *performance* of the industry, in terms of time, cost and quality. These issues are timeless. Although recent examples are mainly used here, similar examples can be found in the classic books by Peck and Scherer (1962) and Scherer (1964).

Although acquisition and procurement are usually synonyms, in defence it is common to distinguish between procurement, which refers only to purchase, and acquisition, which also includes other aspects of ownership. Just as someone purchasing a house has to think about living in it for a long time, someone purchasing a weapon has to think about operating it for a long time. The B-52 bomber has been in service with the US Air Force since 1955 and, in September 2021, Rolls-Royce won a contract to supply aero-engines as part of an upgrade that it is hoped will keep the bombers flying till 2050. The C-130 Hercules military transport aircraft entered service in 1956 and is still in production.

The military love acronyms and the stages of ownership are described in the UK as a CADMID cycle: Concept, Assessment, Demonstration, Manufacture, In-Service and Disposal. Procurement covers ADM, though in the USA the Research, Development, Testing and Evaluation (RDTE) stage is sometimes distinguished from the subsequent procurement stage. In-service operation of equipment is covered by the acronym TEPIDOIL: Training, Equipment, People, Infrastructure, Doctrine, Organisation, Information, Logistics. While most of the elements are self-explanatory, doctrine refers to how the equipment is used and often new technologies are introduced before the military really know how to use them so there is a long period of learning and reorganisation before they are successfully integrated into military doctrine.

The equipment is intended to provide a military capability, though there are many different definitions of capability. Broadly, capability will be used to mean the ability to meet a military objective. There is the difficulty that the primary military objective, prevailing in combat, is difficult to measure in advance, so more quantifiable characteristics of capability are often used. The National Audit Office (NAO 2020b) says the MoD develops and operates military capabilities in order to meet its strategic requirements and objectives. A military capability is not simply a piece of equipment such as a tank. Rather, it is a tank with a trained crew that can: communicate with others on the battlefield; meet identified threats; and be properly maintained and repaired during its lifetime. Giry and Smith (2020) emphasise the role of equipment support in the provision of capability and the different meanings different actors attach to capability.

The various procurement failures have prompted many attempts to fix the problem. Taylor (2019, p. 259) lists eight major reports relating to UK defence procurement between 1961 and 2012, each of which recommended reforms. Fox (2011, p. xi) lists twenty-seven major studies of US defence acquisition. The National Audit Office (NAO 2021) contains recent recommendations for reform in the UK.

While there have been many attempts to fix the problem, the titles of books like *British Weapons Acquisitions Policy and the Futility of Reform* (Chin 2004) and the US study *Defense Acquisition Reform, 1960–2009: An Elusive Goal* (Fox 2011) suggest that the fixes have not worked. The UK Public Accounts Committee (PAC 2021b, pp. 5–6) says of the MoD, 'The Department's system for delivering major equipment capabilities is broken and is repeatedly wasting taxpayers' money. ... The Department continually fails to learn from its mistakes.'

The Foreword to Fox (2011) by Richard Stewart notes how acquisition reform initiatives have been DOD perennials over the past fifty years. Reforming the acquisition process is a high priority each time a new administration comes into office and many studies have reached the same general findings with similar recommendations. But the difficulty of the problem and the associated politics, combined with organisational dynamics that are resistant to change, have led to only minor improvements. He concludes that the problems of schedule slippages, cost growth and shortfalls in technical performance have remained much the same throughout this period.

Fox (2011, p. xiii) lists the built-in cultural aspects that resist change. The workforce frequently does not have the training, experience and stable tenure to monitor and manage huge defence acquisition programmes. The senior, politically appointed acquisition officials average a mere eighteen months in office. There is an irregular and erratic flow of weapons systems appropriations. Risky Research and Development (R&D) and an ill-informed requirements process mean that contracts get changed over time. There are incentives for contractors to bid low. He concludes, 'These cultural challenges within the current acquisition system have great value to many key participants in industry, the services, and Congress and predispose them to be generally resistant to change.'

For the UK, RAND Europe (2021), discussing the underlying causes of equipment procurement problems, highlights a range of issues. A lack of skills and capabilities in industry and the MoD results in poor requirement setting and production inefficiencies. There are problems with supplier performance incentives and contracting. These result in misaligned assumptions and a poor understanding of risk. There is poor programme management, budgeting and delivery. This results in imbalances between the armed services, frequent adjustments to programme delivery management and insufficient risk provision. There are cross-cutting problems like a conspiracy of optimism, lack of institutional memory and moral hazard, issues that will be discussed.

Defence procurement is at a unique interface of politics, technology, warfighting and commerce which can produce conflicting, often perverse, incentives and complicated bureaucratic politics. The account in this Element will emphasise incentives, the interests of the actors, and institutions, the frameworks within which they act.

One incentive shared by nearly all the actors is to be optimistic. This is often called the conspiracy of optimism, but does not require any conspiracy. All the actors – politicians, the military, civil servants and industry – have good reasons to under-estimate the cost and time required for the project and under-state the difficulties it faces. The politician wants to announce an exciting new project, particularly if it generates jobs. The military want the weapon. The civil servants need to spend their budget. The firms want the contract. Thus, it is in their joint and individual interests to make the project look sufficiently attractive to get it into the budgeted plan. Optimism also avoids, or at least postpones, conflicts. The parties may have incompatible demands. For instance, one wants a light armoured vehicle that can be transported by air, one wants it well protected. Rather than exposing the conflict, which may endanger the project's entry into the plan, the parties may agree to avoid the hard choice in the optimistic belief that time or technology will resolve the contradiction. Once the project is in the plan, the hope is that cancellation will be difficult, even if the project fails to meet time, cost and performance targets, and that the system will eventually get into service. Most troubled procurement projects do get into service and turn into operational systems.

It is said that 'where you stand depends on where you sit'; your position on an issue will depend on the organisation that you belong to. In this context, the conspiracy of optimism is an example of 'motivated beliefs'; people believe things that it is in their interests to believe. Their interests influence the way evidence is gathered, the arguments are processed and the memories of past experience are recalled. If salary and promotion depend on believing that 'this time will be different' – that, unlike in the past, high-quality equipment will be procured quickly and cheaply – then there is a good reason to believe it. If, in addition, all the principal actors share this optimism, reinforcing each other's belief, then it is likely that, despite past experience, all will become believers. This effect is likely to be particularly strong if these beliefs will only be proved wrong many years after the crucial decisions have been made, by which time the actors will have moved to other jobs. This is partly the reason that so many reports complain that there is too little institutional learning from experience.

There are many forms of organisation that can be used to perform an economic function such as buying weapons. For instance, the function can be provided within a hierarchical organisation like a firm or government, or provided through an arm's-length market relationship. A firm may have a choice between making a component itself or buying it from an outside supplier. Economists often explain the make-or-buy choice in terms of what they call 'transaction costs'. The perceived transaction costs associated with negotiating with outside parties influence the form of organisation that the government chooses to provide the weapons.

Transaction costs are likely to be low if the procurement involves the frequent purchase of a standard commodity from a competitive market. High transaction costs provide incentives to produce in-house, through arsenals or state-owned arms firms. Transaction costs will be higher if there is 'asset specificity' – the facility can only be used for supplying the defence department – which creates mutual dependency between the defence department and the firm. Transaction costs increase with uncertainty, which makes it more difficult to write a contract with a private firm that will cover all eventualities. As transaction costs fall, the weapons may be produced in partnership with a private firm under a cost-plus profit partnership; they may be produced in government-owned facilities by a private firm; or they may be procured competitively with a fixed-price contract, as is common in commercial markets. The Department of Defense (DOD 2022, p. 3) notes that in 2021, by number of contracts, 90 per cent of the contracts awarded were competed for, but most of them were small; by value of contracts, only 52 per cent of the dollars awarded followed competition; and in major weapons systems, competition rates ranged from 15 to 40 per cent.

1.1 Market Structure

The structure of the market reflects the nature of demand and supply. On the demand side is the government defence department that buys the weapons. How much it wants to spend on weapons will reflect its budget constraint (its ability to pay); its perception of national interests and threats to those interests; and the opportunity costs of the military expenditure (what has to be given up to fund defence). Defence departments buy a very wide variety of products. There are standard civilian products like fuel, food and clothing; military products like small arms, major conventional weapons systems and weapons of mass destruction; and dual-use products like communications, crypto- and cyber-systems.

The focus of this Element is on major weapons systems, like aircraft, ships and armoured vehicles. Defence departments are major buyers of oil products – aircraft, ships and armoured vehicles use a lot of fuel – but oil does not raise any special issues because there is a large civilian market for oil. Like civil airlines, defence departments outside the USA have to consider whether they should hedge against variations in the price of oil and equipment, both of which are usually priced in dollars. The UK MoD uses forward (swap) contracts to hedge against the oil price and hedges equipment import costs with the Bank of England. But such hedging choices are not specifically military. The special issues arise in the market for major weapons systems, which has characteristics that are different from civilian markets.

The government is usually the only national buyer for major weapons systems, though there may be export markets. Having a single buyer is called monopsony. Not only are governments usually the only domestic customer but they are also often: an investor, financing R&D; an export regulator, determining where the weapons can be sold; a marketing manager for the overseas sales; and an owner, since many arms companies are state-owned.

On the supply side is the arms industry that makes the weapons. Defining the arms industry is difficult and arms are not a category in any of the standard lists, such as UN Standard International Trade Classification (SITC). Both military and civilian items are included in many of the relevant categories, such as aerospace and electronic equipment. There is also a large amount of dual-use equipment, which can have both military and civilian applications. These measurement issues are sufficiently difficult that what seem like simple quantities, such as the number employed in the arms industry or the value of defence exports, are difficult to measure. There may be no measure available or many conflicting measures differing with respect to the exact definition or the method of calculation.

At one level major weapons systems are relatively easy to identify as an aircraft, tank or warship. Yet at another level they are complex products which combine a lot of elements. There is a platform, such as the aircraft; its armaments, such as missiles; its avionics, such as communications and radar; and its logistics, which ensure its supplies and keep it operational. An aircraft needs a large team on the ground. This means that there may be considerable uncertainty about exactly what is being purchased and what it costs, depending on what is included in the total.

The development of new major weapons systems often involves the use of untested technologies against uncertain and evolving threats. Smaller, simpler military contracts have fewer failures or fewer failures that get publicity. Production of weapons systems usually involves large R&D expenditures and there are other fixed costs which have to be spread over each unit. Thus, the average cost of each unit falls with the number produced. There are also learning curves, where the marginal production cost of each additional unit falls. Both result in increasing returns to scale, which can make competition not viable. The more a firm can produce, the lower its costs, making smaller producers uncompetitive, leaving only a single seller that can profitably survive. Increasing returns to scale also make exporting attractive, to spread the fixed costs and gain the benefit of learning curves.

1.2 Conduct

The main elements of conduct involve the behaviour of the buyers and sellers in the procurement and acquisition of weapons. Given the long time-horizons, uncertainty is central. The uncertainty may be about supply – will the technology work? – or about demand – what will the future requirement be? The Eurofighter Typhoon was designed for air superiority in the early 1980s, reflecting Cold War needs. When it came into service in the mid-2000s it was re-equipped for ground attack roles. It could still be operating in the 2040s, facing quite different demands. The uncertainty complicates decision-making, both for the buyer, about what is wanted, and for the buyer and supplier, about how it should be provided.

The interaction between a single buyer and relatively few potential suppliers involves a lot of political economy issues, the nature of the defence department and any military-industrial complex, as well as what are called *principal-agent problems*. These include asymmetric information, risk aversion, moral hazard and adverse selection. They are discussed in Section 5. The terms *moral hazard* and *adverse selection* are taken from insurance. Providing fire insurance might create an incentive for the insured to start a fire to collect on the insurance. That is moral hazard. The insurance may attract only those at most risk of being subject to fires. That is adverse selection. In economics, they are used in a wider sense, as will become apparent.

Whereas the principal-agent issue is a two-level problem, between government and firm, there is a three-level problem: government, defence department as regulator and firm. Regulatory capture is the term used by economists for the process by which special interests, such as a military-industrial complex, capture the regulator, the defence department, so the regulator is not necessarily doing what the government intends. Dal Bó (2006) reviews regulatory capture.

Neither the government nor the defence department are unitary decision-makers. Within the defence department, procurement and acquisition involve a large number of complex coalitions of different warring tribes with different interests and cultures. The tribes, which are discussed in Section 6, include the politicians, the different armed services and civilian government employees. The civilians may be administrators, trying to keep the projects running smoothly; strategic specialists in the intelligence community forecasting future threats; scientists and engineers, designing the weapons; lawyers, advising on the contracts with the firms; financial experts, advising on the terms; and many other specialists. Inter-service rivalry between the army, navy and air force for an increased share of the budget is continuous. Each tribe will have its own language and experience, making it difficult for them to communicate with each other even when they do not strategically hoard information in their own silo. Watters (2019) has a nice description of the cultural competition between the tribes in the UK MoD and Akam (2021) between the tribes in the UK army.

Many of the government actors in the procurement process, including the military, may be in post for relatively short times since it is common to rotate personnel through different two-year postings. For different reasons, the people in charge may also have short tenures. In the twenty years to November 2021, the UK had eleven Secretaries of State for Defence, the USA nine Secretaries of Defense plus five acting Secretaries of Defense. The US Secretaries mostly had a background in defence. Many of the UK Secretaries, who have to be chosen from Members of Parliament, had relatively little knowledge of defence before taking up the role. In some countries, the elected representatives have a detailed role in budgeting, as in the US Congress. In other countries, the elected representatives have a relatively limited role, as in the UK Parliament.

Other institutions are involved, like the NAO in the UK and GAO in the USA, who have auditing functions. Another institution of particular importance is the finance ministry. There is usually tension between the defence department, which spends money, and the finance ministry, which tries to control spending. In the UK, the finance ministry, known as Her Majesty's Treasury, has always been seen as the number one enemy in the MoD. Hennessy (2003, p. 196) describes how, in the event of a nuclear war, Project Turnstile would evacuate, to a bunker beneath the Cotswolds, the 210 people thought needed to keep the UK running. Project Turnstile was organised by the MoD, which did not include anyone from the Treasury on the passenger list.

Inter-service rivalry, political-military tensions and disputes between the defence department and other organisations like the finance ministry and auditors all complicate decision-making about requirements and timing.

1.3 Performance in Procurement

Consider now some examples of poor performance in the procurement of major weapons systems. The F-35, for which Lockheed Martin is the prime contractor, began development in 2001 and first flew in 2006. In the USA, the Nunn-McCurdy Act requires the DOD to report to Congress whenever a Major Defense Acquisition Program experiences cost overruns that exceed certain thresholds. The F-35 breached these thresholds in 2009, when costs had doubled. There are three variants. The conventional F-35A entered service with the US Air Force in 2016; the short take-off/vertical landing F-35B with the Marine Corps in 2015; and the carrier-based F-35C with the US Navy in 2019. Concurrent production and development caused problems and there is still a large number of technical problems. In July 2021 the GAO (2021) said, 'Currently, the program is 8 years delayed and $165 billion over original cost expectations. As the program progresses towards completing operational testing of the aircraft's baseline capabilities, it still faces risks.' By the end of 2021, 753 had been produced, even though it had not completed the operational testing usually required before an aircraft goes into full production. Its much higher operation and support costs than the aircraft it replaced were also a source of concern. The Congressional Research Service (CRS 2022) provides a history of the development of the F-35.

The US Future Combat Systems (FCS) was launched in 2003. The vision was to create army brigades equipped with new crewed and autonomous vehicles linked by an unprecedented, fast and flexible battlefield network. Thirty-two billion dollars were expended on this programme, with little to show for it. In 2009, it was cancelled. Although a number of examples of cancellation will be mentioned, it is quite rare for a major failing project to be stopped. Projects are easy to begin but difficult and expensive to stop. The pattern is for things to go wrong, the project is reviewed, some changes are made and the project proceeds in the hope that the problems are not sufficiently serious to stop the system going into service.

Armoured vehicles have been equally problematic in the UK with programmes also cancelled. The House of Commons Defence Committee (HCDC 2021) produced a report, *Obsolescent and Outgunned: The British Army's Armoured Vehicle Capability*, which 'reveals a woeful story of bureaucratic procrastination, military indecision, financial mismanagement and general ineptitude, which have continually bedevilled attempts to properly re-equip the British Army over the last two decades'. Frequent changes in personnel within project teams and a lack of ingrained technical knowledge and understanding of armoured vehicle development resulting from the transfer of design authority to industry in the 1990s were also cited as contributing factors to the failure to deliver new vehicles to the Army.

The Warrior infantry fighting vehicle came into service in 1984. In February 2010, the Warrior programme team sought approval from the MoD Investment Approvals Committee (IAC) to proceed to the demonstration phase of an upgrade. The upgrade was ultimately approved in October 2011. During this period, the estimated date of entry into service slipped from 2014 to 2020. In response to updates in 2016 and 2018, the IAC asked the team to provide a clear statement of the programme's value for money (VFM) in the forthcoming request for approval to manufacture but this submission continued to slip. In February 2019, the accounting officer provided an assessment of the programme to the Committee of Public Accounts. This stated that it was too early to conclude on the programme's VFM, but the available evidence was that the current solution still offered the 'best VFM'.

In the UK the Infrastructure and Projects Authority (IPA) was set up in 2016 to provide expert project delivery advice, support and assurance to government departments and work with industry to ensure projects are delivered efficiently and effectively, and to improve performance over time. In October 2020, the IPA advised that a proper VFM assessment was still not possible and it was therefore still too soon to seek approval for the manufacture stage. As at December 2020, the programme team expected to achieve initial operating capability in 2026 and full operating capability in 2028, and expected to have spent over £580 million on the programme by March 2021. The upgrade involved fitting a new turret equipped with a cannon supplied under a separate contract. This left the MoD with the challenging task of integrating the contribution of a range of suppliers and providing key components as Government Furnished Assets to the lead contractor, Lockheed Martin. The lead supplier and the supplier of the cannon were not in a contractual relationship although their work was interdependent. In March 2021, the government announced in the Integrated Review of Security, Defence, Development and Foreign Policy that it had cancelled the upgrade programme.

There were also problems with another UK armoured fighting vehicle, Ajax, which was a development of an existing vehicle used in other countries. The MoD signed a contract with the US defence contractor General Dynamics (GD) in March 2010. The contract was for a family of 589 vehicles worth £5.5 billion in total, which would be assembled in South Wales and GD promised 10,000 jobs. As of 2021, when the problems were publicised, £3.5 billion had been paid. Delivery should have started in 2017 but trials were halted over concerns that noise and vibration were damaging crews' hearing. Again there was an issue with a separate contract for the cannon and the MoD required further armour. Changing specifications in the course of a contract is a common feature of defence procurement. At the time of writing it is not clear whether the project will be cancelled. Taylor (2022, p. 2) describes the problems with this programme and comments: 'Many defence budgets overrun their schedules and budgets, and do not fulfil all their requirements. However, it is rare for an order to go into production that is fundamentally unsafe for its crews and simply not fit for purpose.'

As another UK example, NAO (2020a) reported on three nuclear infrastructure projects on sites subject to oversight by various nuclear regulators. These projects provide the facilities to build the submarines, their nuclear propulsion systems and the nuclear warheads to arm them. In each case the contractor for the project is a monopoly supplier. The first project involves building new facilities at the BAE owned and operated shipyard in Barrow to allow a modular build approach for the Dreadnought submarines. The second project involves replacing facilities at a Rolls-Royce owned and operated site in Derby to produce the latest design of nuclear reactor core for submarine propulsion. The third project involves building a new nuclear warhead assembly and disassembly facility at the MoD owned and Atomic Weapons Establishment (AWE) operated site in Burghfield (Reading). This is what is known as a GoCo (government-owned, contractor-operated) relationship. The contractor was a joint venture between Serco (24.5 per cent), Lockheed Martin (51 per cent) and Jacobs (24.5 per cent). In November 2020 the MoD announced that AWE would be renationalised from June 2021.

None of the three nuclear infrastructure projects will be delivered to their original timeframe, with delays of between 1.7 and 6.3 years and a combined cost increase of £1.35 billion over budget. The NAO concluded that the MoD failed to learn from the experience with the early stages of similar projects in the UK and elsewhere and it had made the same mistakes as it had made thirty years earlier. These included starting to build before requirements or designs were sufficiently mature, increasing risks through inappropriate contracts and failing to engage with regulators to understand requirements. Some of these challenges were also identified in UK civil projects and US defence projects. Many – including MoD-wide projects – were subject to extensive reviews, but NAO could not identify examples of the MoD formally capturing and sharing lessons learned (NAO 2020a, p. 7).

There is an argument that characterising these projects as failures can miss the point that military and civilian standards of efficiency may be very different. Luttwak (1985, p. 139), in his chapter 'Why We Need More Fraud, Waste and Mismanagement in the Pentagon', says: 'But when it comes to material power, the relationship between material inputs and desired outputs is not proportional;

it is in fact very loose, because the making of military strength is dominated by the nonmaterial, quite intangible human factors, from the quality of national military strategy to the fighting morale of individual servicemen.' He also says: 'The trouble is that the outputs that count in war are very particular and very different from the outputs that count in peacetime and when civilian notions of efficiency are applied, the difference is routinely overlooked' (p. 133). This issue of the difficulty of measuring defence output will recur in Section 3, which is concerned with costs.

1.4 Concluding Comments

Procurement failures are not confined to weapons systems. Berlin's Brandenburg Airport opened in autumn 2020, ten years late, and cost at least €7 billion, two and a half times its original budget. London's Crossrail, Boston's Big Dig and Hanoi's Metro were similarly late and over budget. They are characteristic of what have been labelled megaprojects, government or commercial. Flyvbjerg (2014) identifies four temptations that lead to failure in megaprojects. There is a technological sublime: the rapture that engineers and technologists get from building large and innovative projects; a political sublime: the rapture politicians get from building monuments to themselves; an economic sublime: the delight business people and trade unions receive from the profits and jobs created; an aesthetic sublime: the pleasure got from building, using and looking at something beautiful. These same temptations often lurk behind big military projects. The weapons are often innovative monuments, which politicians can promote as generating jobs and profits and which can even seem beautiful to their admirers. Sometimes it appears that weapons are bought not because they are effective but because they are cool.

Such failures are not even confined to big projects. Anyone who has hired builders for home improvements or repairs will know that the project often takes longer than expected, costs more than the budget and is not quite what was hoped for. Renovating a house involves similar levels of uncertainty to procuring a weapon. It is not known what shortcuts were taken by the previous owner's cheap builder or what will be revealed once the cladding is removed. Relationships between householders and builders can be as fraught as those between defence departments and prime contractors. Home improvement has many of the characteristics of defence procurement and the analogy will recur.

Failure to meet time, cost and performance targets is not peculiar to the military and many smaller, more routine military projects are completed efficiently. However, as will be seen, major weapons systems have a range of characteristics that makes their procurement and acquisition difficult.

2 Requirements: What Weapons Are Needed?

In deciding what to purchase a defence department has to ask: what can be afforded? what should the weapon do? and when is it needed? There are trade-offs between the three elements; quicker delivery and higher quality come at a cost. In peacetime, the military tend to put quality first, cost second and time third. In combat, the ranking changes dramatically and time becomes of the essence. Rather than a dilemma, where one must choose between two desirable outcomes, there is a trilemma; one can only have at most two of the three desirable outcomes: good, quick and cheap. But there are strong incentives for the decision-makers to be optimistic and to believe that an unrealistic combination of performance, timetable and budget is possible.

The USA systematised decision-making in the 1960s through the Planning, Programming and Budgeting System (PPBS). This involves balancing marginal security benefits against opportunity costs after evaluating the likely threats; choosing the appropriate technology; managing the quantity–quality trade-off; and determining the time-horizon for delivery. The literature on these choices poses the classic questions: 'How much is enough?' and 'How to get the biggest bang for a buck?'

Some military thinkers present strategy as the combination of ends, ways and means. The ends are what you want to achieve; the ways are the actions that will enable you to achieve your ends; and the means are the resources you need to take those actions. While this framework has its limitations, it can be used to organise the elements that go into requirements.

2.1 Ends

In determining the desired ends, optimal defence planning is often seen as a process of thinking forward and reasoning back. Think forward to the possible *threats* to national interests and security then reason back to work out the ways, the *capabilities* (military or otherwise) needed to deter those threats or defend against them. Next calculate the *forces* (personnel, equipment and infrastructure) needed to provide the required capabilities and finally the means, the *budget* needed to fund those forces. At the optimum, the budget balances the value of the possible security gains from defence against the benefits from the alternative uses of the money, its opportunity cost.

Thus, in determining optimal defence policy, the questions that need to be answered by a country are:

- What is its role in the world and its associated national interests?
- What are the most likely threats to its homeland and to its interests or commitments overseas?
- What are the most effective military responses to those threats?
- What forces are needed to provide that response and what support can be expected from allies?
- How much will the forces cost?
- When will the costs be incurred?

The answer to each of these questions is, of course, 'We cannot know'. Given the lack of information, optimisation against expected threats can prove inadequate when the unexpected threats materialise. Then policy just has to muddle through. In addition, force structures are conservative, hard to change. This is partly inertia but partly caution. If a weapons system has proved useful in the past it seems dangerous to abandon it. As a result, the *follow-on imperative* is very strong. It is bureaucratically easier to replace an existing type of system, such as piloted aircraft, than to drop that type and invest in a completely new type, such as autonomous aerial vehicles, not yet in service. The new type may provide the same type of capability as the old or provide a completely different type of capability, losing the capability that the old system provided. There were lots of things cavalry could do that tanks could not do. In this bureaucratic battle the old type has the advantage of a large constituency with an interest in defending it, which the new type does not.

There is a constellation of potentially hostile state and non-state actors, who may target the UK for various reasons in economic, political or military arenas, using kinetic, hybrid or digital tactics, in land, maritime, air, space or cyber dimensions. Innovations like improvised explosive devices or small drones, which provide relatively cheap forms of attack but are expensive to defend against, are particularly problematic. Threats come not just from hostile actors but also from nature, like climate change, pollution and pandemics. Many decisions, like the decision as to what role the Chinese company Huawei should be allowed to play in the provision of 5G, involve trading off geostrategic, geopolitical and geoeconomic dimensions.

During defence reviews, politicians, civil servants and the military strive to clarify foreign policy objectives, identify a range of plausible risks and threats, and formulate defence policies to counter the threats that are most likely or most dangerous. But despite this hard work they are very likely to be overtaken by events not predicted in the plan. This is not to say planning is futile. There is the military saying: 'failing to plan is planning to fail'. But there is the other military saying, 'no plan survives contact with the enemy'. Therefore one needs to build in adaptability and resilience to be able to cope with the unexpected, but this can be expensive.

UK defence planning after 1945 focused on fighting the Soviet Union and then Russia within the NATO area. But the UK fought almost anybody but them: the North Koreans and Chinese, lots of now ex-colonies, the Irish, the Argentinians, the Iraqis and the Afghans among others. Not knowing who you will have to fight is nothing new. These were all 'Come as you are' wars, fought with whatever was available. While there was some consideration of 'out of area' operations in the requirements process, these wars were not fought with equipment geared to those particular threats.

The effect of unpredictability on the equipment requirement is illustrated by UK defence reviews, described in HCL (2020). The 1981 Nott Review planned to scrap a range of naval assets. This had not yet been implemented when the Falklands/Malvinas were invaded in 1982 and these assets were crucial in the subsequent war. Had Argentina waited another six months, the ships might have been scrapped and the UK would not have been able to assemble the task force that retook the islands. The post–Cold War, July 1990, *Options for Change* review was followed by the August 1990 Iraqi invasion of Kuwait and the unanticipated 1991 Gulf War. The 2015 review *Making Defence International by Design* did not allow for the effect of Brexit on our allies.

2.2 Ways

Ways cover the actions needed to achieve ends, the specific choices about how to fight and the weapons needed to fight with. In the UK, the requirement process is informed by a process of combined operational effectiveness and investment appraisal (COEIA) to judge the cost-effectiveness of alternative equipment options. This is described in Kirkpatrick (1996). Specifying requirements is difficult because stakeholders differ over what is needed, and what is needed changes as uncertainties in technology are resolved and the perceived threat changes. US and UK combat experience in Afghanistan and Iraq showed that the threat from improvised explosive devices (IED) was more serious than expected and equipment had to be adapted rapidly to take account of this new threat.

There is a choice between presenting open requirements as a set of 'cardinal points' – the general objectives of the system, what the weapon is supposed to do – as against detailed requirements about how it should meet those objectives. RAND Europe (2021) reported that the MoD response to the uncertainties inherent in weapons development has often been to specify prescriptive requirements that solicited an ambitious, 'gold-plated' proposal from industry. Where technical specifications are set out in too much detail, instead of, for example, setting out the broad military requirements, industry has little room for manoeuvre in defining how the requirement could be delivered in the most efficient and effective way. The UK Defence and Security Accelerator (DASA) is also trying to establish a more open system. It is modelled on the US Defense Advanced Research Projects Agency (DARPA), which has effectively used competitions, such as for self-driving vehicles, where only the end is specified. But defence departments also have to ensure that the equipment will integrate into the rest of the system all the TEPIDOIL elements (Training, Equipment, People, Infrastructure, Doctrine, Organisation, Information, Logistics) which may require detailed specifications.

Howell et al. (2021) describe the benefits of open requirements to the US Air Force. The paper argues that US defence R&D increasingly lags behind the private sector, partly because innovation procurement is narrowly specified and located in a small group of defence specialist firms, leaving little room for more radical thinking. It provides evidence that the US defence sector has been growing less innovative compared with the rest of the US economy since the early 1990s, a period which coincides with extensive merger and acquisition (M&A) activity that consolidated the defence industry. From the DOD's perspective, it is problematic if the best technologies are no longer marketed to the military. To address these issues, the Air Force experimented with open topics in certain of its contracts starting in 2018. The goals of open topics are to reach non-traditional firms with frontier dual-use technology and to source ideas that the Air Force may not yet know it needs. Requirements can evolve as the technology does; these are known as agile contracts and can be difficult to manage.

There is an issue as to who should make the decision about what is wanted. In particular, should it be the military or procurement professionals? While their input is important, it is not clear that the military have the skills required for procurement, which include knowledge of the relevant science, engineering and technology and the management, financial and commercial expertise needed for planning, budgeting and negotiating with contractors. The skills required in combat and the skills required in project management are very different. Although the US military has experimented with hiring specialist procurement contracting officers, it is unlikely that most officers joined the military for a career in engineering or accounting. There is the danger that the military are likely to be over-influenced by the last war they fought or the last equipment they used. Their posting to procurement is likely to be quite short, perhaps two years, and their promotion depends more on loyalty to service values than on the success of the project they are temporarily posted to. This issue is discussed further in Section 6 in the context of a comparison of the British and French procurement systems.

Whether the requirements are specified by the military or procurement professionals, the defence department needs to be a well-informed customer in dealing with industry and understand the potential of technology and materials. This is the role of the Defence Technology Base (DTB). The DTB should identify and assess emerging threats, help to formulate a requirement for equipment to counter those threats, compare proposals from alternative suppliers, assist domestic suppliers to develop, manufacture and support the chosen equipment, and test and evaluate the equipment when delivered. To do this requires a strong scientific base and a suitable R&D budget. Taylor (2022), commenting on the lessons from the Ajax programme, says, 'if government runs down its in-house expertise, it must rely on corporate claims about what is possible in a period of time for a fixed sum of money. Yet, especially in a competitive context, companies can be driven towards excessive optimism in their offers.'

Time may be of the essence. In combat, an expensive piece of equipment which hardly meets the requirement but is available now may be of much more value than a cheaper, more effective alternative that will be available in the future. Procurement tends to be divided between normal budgeted procurement and requirements needed rapidly in war. In the UK the latter are called urgent operational requirements (UORs) and in the USA are covered by emergency supplemental funds. Normal procurement processes are slow (seven years on average), formalised and encompass many objectives. They try to build compatibility with the rest of the system to minimise maintenance costs and maximise inter-operability and usually require R&D. UORs are fast (usually less than six months), informal, focus on a single objective, may be incompatible with the rest of the system (creating fleets within fleets) and largely use off-the-shelf components. During wars UORs can be acquired and put into service very rapidly. During the 1982 Falklands War the UK got AIM-9 L Sidewinder air-to-air missiles from the United States at 48 hours' notice. They were taken from US aircraft and fitted to the UK Harrier aircraft very quickly. Similarly, in 2006 US Marine Corps Cougar armoured vehicles, renamed Mastiff by the British, went directly to British troops in Iraq.

Akam (2021, chapter 16) provides an account of the use of UORs by the British Army to provide equipment, including new camouflage, for use in Iraq and Afghanistan, with quotations from many of those involved. PAC (2005) reported that a third of the UORs to support the war-fighting phases of operations in Iraq were to fill previously identified gaps in capability which the MoD considered too low a priority to fund from its regular procurement budget.

These were cases where overspends on the large projects crowded out smaller valuable items. Finance ministries are inevitably concerned that the military may regard UORs as free money and the Treasury raised a number of objections to particular projects. There were also disputes about whether the equipment would be retained, in which case it would come out of the regular budget. Accounting procedures can be important.

Given a fixed budget, there is a choice between the quality and quantity of weapons: a few technologically advanced, highly capable units or many less capable units. The choice of the number of units also has implications for the number of armed forces required to operate and maintain them. The balance between quality and quantity will be chosen to maximise force effectiveness, which depends both on the number of units and the capability of each. This quantity–quality balance is often described by Lanchester Laws, after Frederick Lanchester who in 1916 developed mathematical models of the relative power of opposing forces. Kirkpatrick (2021) examines Lanchester Laws and the importance of superior numbers in a historical context, using data from the American Civil War. He concludes that the number of fighting units is less important than the ability of those units to get into action and inflict losses on the enemy. Arreguin-Toft (2005) uses a large range of historical examples to examine how the weak win wars through the use of asymmetric conflict: using different strategies from the strong actor and not allowing the strong actor to employ their extra resources effectively.

One solution to the quantity/quality dilemma is to maintain a hi-low mix, as the USA does by combining small numbers of the expensive F-15 aircraft with large numbers of the cheaper F-16. The F-16, being a relatively cheap aircraft, has also been successful in export markets; almost 5,000 have been produced with about half going abroad. It has sometimes been argued that export potential should be built into the process of specifying requirements. There is a tension here. The main producers of major weapons systems are major military powers acquiring high-end systems designed to fight each other. These systems are expensive, thus reducing their export potential. Choosing cheaper designs to boost export potential, as the French have done on occasion, risks fielding a less capable variant than the country needs, leaving the military feeling under-equipped.

One way around this tension is to sell equipment to be used for a different purpose than the one for which it is designed. The BAE Hawk and Dassault/ Dornier Alpha Jet were designed as fast jet trainers, the Hawk for the UK Royal Air Force and the Alpha Jet for France and Germany. Equipped with munitions, both were widely exported as combat aircraft. In both cases the design included the capability to carry munitions, a capability not required in a trainer. The Hawk had begun as a private venture and the company, who financed the development, built in the capability to give it export potential. The Alpha Jet was intended by Germany to be used in combat operation. Over 900 Hawks and 500 Alpha Jets have been produced, mostly for export in both cases. A variant of the Hawk was used as a trainer by the US Navy. Both seem to have been developed without major problems, perhaps because they were relatively simple aircraft. When Germany retired the Alpha Jet, many were sold on to other countries. Such resale is another way to resolve the tension between the demand by the main producers for high-cost, capable equipment and demand in the export markets for low-cost equipment for a low-threat environment. Exports of used equipment, retired from service by the major powers, is a significant part of exports of major weapons systems.

There may be a choice between investing in new systems or upgrading old ones. Upgrading, by technology insertion, may be attractive when military effectiveness depends not on the characteristics of the platform – aircraft, ship or tank – but on what it carries – sensors, weapons or electronics, which can be upgraded within the old platform, as in the B-52. However, fitting new kit into old platforms can be like putting new wine in old bottles, making mid-life upgrades expensive, as the Warrior upgrade discussed in Section 1 illustrates.

In many cases the crucial military capability is not the possession of particular equipment but the possession of particular organisational skills and social architectures that enable the armed services to operate effectively in a crisis. Often the equipment required has not been procured and has to be bought quickly, off-the-shelf, to satisfy urgent operational requirements. It may be acquired either from military sources, like the Sidewinder missiles for the Falklands, or from civilian sources, like the commercial Global Positioning System (GPS) receivers for the 1991 Gulf War. However, general-purpose engineering and scientific skills were needed to fit Sidewinders to Harriers and GPS to vehicles.

Investment in major weapons systems may not only be unnecessary on occasion but also counterproductive, if paying for the big optimised equipment becomes a black hole devouring the budget, leaving little left over for basics. To use UK examples, there is the danger that in conflict it is discovered that the basics are either inadequate, like army boots in the Falklands or Snatch Land Rovers in Iraq, or are in short supply, like body armour in Iraq. Similarly, spending on large naval warships optimised for Blue Water power projection may leave little money for the smaller vessels needed for other missions. In the UK case these may include fishery protection after Brexit or stopping illegal immigrants crossing the channel, for which the ships absorbing the budget are unsuitable. An argument might be made that the basics can be easily acquired when we go to war, as were the 'Ships Taken Up From Trade' for the Falklands War, whereas the big optimised equipment has to be procured well in advance. But, like PPE in the pandemic or the 155 mm ammunition from Belgium during the Gulf War, supply of the basics may not be available when needed. This is a particular problem when supply is dependent on political decisions by allies. Returning to the Sidewinder example, the Reagan administration was deeply divided over the Falklands so it is conceivable that missiles might not have been made available so quickly.

2.3 Means

Means are the resources needed to take the action that will enable the ends to be achieved. The resources are financed primarily from the defence budget. Government budgeting procedures are invariably complex and differ between countries. Defence budgets can be large. The Biden administration requested $715 billion in discretionary budget authority for the DOD in fiscal year 2022. This amounts to almost half of the total discretionary spending requested for that fiscal year. Discretionary spending is distinct from mandatory spending that is legally required. The UK defence budget for 2022 is about $68 billion; the French defence budget about $48 billion. There are some differences in the definition of the defence budget in the three countries. The budget constraint limits the amount of money which can be spent on defence and there are opportunity costs within the budget: purchasing a particular piece of equipment means the money cannot be spent on other aspects of capability. Cost overruns on one project displace other, perhaps more valuable, projects.

There is a tension between the long-term nature of procurement, where projects and contracts last many years or decades, and the short-term nature of financial control through the annual budget cycle. The amount authorised to be spent by the defence department in a fiscal year may be supplemented by, for instance, the additional costs incurred in an unanticipated conflict. There are longer term budgets: the US five-year spending plan, the Future Years Defense Program, and the UK ten-year Equipment Plan. However, given the fallibility of forecasts, these documents are treated by many as works of fiction.

There are two sources of strain on the budget: external and internal. The external strain arises from fluctuations in the budget when planned spending has to be cut because economic circumstances require reductions in government expenditure. The internal strain arises from under-estimation of costs, which means that not all the planned procurement can be afforded. This may be moderated a little by under-estimation of time required so the costs arrive later than expected, allowing some breathing space or even under-spending on occasion. These two sources of strain have disrupted equipment procurement in many countries. When lack of funds causes cuts in quantities procured or delays in production, it can raise unit cost substantially.

These strains on the budget cause imbalances between commitments, capabilities and resources. This has been a particular problem for the UK since World War II. These persistent imbalances are temporarily resolved by defence reviews, typically prompted by economic crisis, which cut capabilities in an attempt to balance the budget. The main reviews were Sandys 1957, Healey 1965–8, Mason 1974–5, Nott 1981, *Options for Change* 1990, the Strategic Defence Review 1998, Strategic Defence and Security Review 2010, Strategic Defence and Security Review 2015 and the Integrated Review of 2021. A description of the earlier reviews is provided in HCL (2020). Of the post-war defence reviews, only those of 1998 and 2015 were not associated with economic crises. The reviews resolve the issues for the moment but are typically over-ambitious and under-funded so the problems recur. Some have criticised these reviews for being budget-driven rather than threat-driven, but these are two sides of the same coin. Reviews have to trade off the opportunity costs of budget increases against the security benefits of threat reduction.

The Public Accounts Committee (PAC 2021a, p. 10) *Report on Equipment Plan* reported that the Permanent Secretary, the most senior civil servant,

> told us that in 2010 the defence budget had been made affordable, but at the expense of capability. Then in 2015, capability shortfalls were addressed but without sufficient funding. The budget was, therefore, constantly unbalanced in one way or another. He told us that he hoped now to develop a coherent and sensible package of capabilities which are backed up by resources, allowing the Department to plan properly in the longer term.

The imbalance between budgets, capabilities and commitments has been a recurring theme in the defence policy of the UK and other countries. Not enough money was provided to enable the military to do properly what had been promised, though whether the problem was the provision or the promises is disputed.

2.4 Concluding Comments

To return to the housing example, similar issues about requirements arise between partners confronting the need to do work on their house. One may see this as an opportunity to spend their savings on renovating the house; the other thinks they should just do the minimal repairs required and spend the rest on a holiday to renovate themselves. Both have incentives to hope for the best and under-estimate how much the building work is going to cost.

The householders have to choose a builder to meet their requirements and establish their priorities. The honest builder will say, 'I can do quality, I can do quick and I can do cheap, but not all three: choose two'.

Setting requirements in the face of unpredictable threats and unknown technology may turn out to be an impossible task of optimising against unknowns. Given this, a common analogy is to treat defence policy as an insurance policy. A country does not know what may occur so it pays a premium: a defence budget of some percentage of its income, its gross domestic product (GDP), which is invested in such a way that it pays off by reducing damage if something nasty does occur. The investments are in various sorts of military capabilities and they may pay off in ways that could not be predicted in advance, including in support of the civil power, such as building hospitals and organising medical tests in a pandemic. As in ordinary insurance, there is a choice about how much cover is purchased: what uncertain events are insured against; the wider the cover, the higher the premium. Before both World Wars I and II, UK defence policy did not prepare for committing forces to a major Continental conflict so was under-insured.

The UK military have argued that while the government has only been willing to pay the premiums for basic 'third party, fire and theft' insurance, it has tried repeatedly to claim on the policy as if they had paid for 'fully comprehensive' insurance. Since the military tend to have a 'can do' attitude, they try to respond to these claims, even if the defence policy did not cover them. In consequence, the services suffer overstretch and face big risks in unplanned operations, like the Falklands, Basra and Helmand, that were never included in the strategic ends.

3 Price: What Will the Weapons Cost?

Economists think of cost or expenditure as the product of price times quantity. But, in defence, life is not that simple. There are many measures of expenditure depending on what is included. While there may be simple measures of quantity, like the number of aircraft, the technical characteristics of the aircraft change over time and it may not be clear how the number of aircraft relates to defence output (the quantity of defence they provide). Not only is measuring costs difficult but there are various different aspects of cost growth that might be of interest: between generations of weapons system, over the lifetime of a project and for the defence budget as a whole. Each of these aspects will be considered in turn.

The initial costs of a weapons system include R&D, tooling, production, testing and initial support. Whole-life costs also include operations, in-service support and disposal. Measurement of costs, particularly whole-life costs, is difficult even after the event. There are questions about how to allocate joint costs to particular projects. R&D, facilities, capital equipment and other overheads may be used to support many projects. This becomes even more difficult when the system is in operation with the armed forces. It is often not clear which elements of the system are included in the cost number. It might be just the platform, or platform plus armaments plus communications plus other elements, like support and training. Given that measurement after the event is difficult, forecasting before procurement is even more hazardous.

Bongers and Torres (2014) discuss the issues in measuring the price of a fighter aircraft. The 'flyaway cost' is the unit production cost. This excludes RDTE costs, which are considered sunk costs, other supplementary costs, such as support costs, and future costs, such as spares and maintenance costs. 'Procurement cost' adds to flyaway cost the cost of the development programme divided by the number of aircraft produced, which is not known till the end of production. When R&D spending contributes to a number of different projects, there are issues of how it should be allocated to each. There are learning curves so production cost drops as the number produced increases, meaning flyaway cost is not constant. To control for this, they use the flyaway cost of the hundredth unit, when most learning has ceased, to make the prices comparable.

There are parametric cost estimation procedures. These use past information on how costs are related to characteristics of the system, such as cost per kilogramme of aircraft delivered, to provide estimates. They are approximate, as each system is unique, but can be quite useful, particularly in identifying where some break in trend is assumed in the cost estimate. Kirkpatrick (2019) comments on costing that a whole-life approach is easiest to implement if the capital asset acquired uses a mature technology and operates in a predictable environment but is much more difficult if the asset uses a new technology, has a long life cycle or operates in an unpredictable environment, all characteristics of major weapons systems. There are benefits in integrating design, production and support in order to minimise the whole-life costs. Aero-engine manufacturers sell 'power by the hour': they are paid for the hours operated by the engine and take responsibility for them. In normal times civil aero-engine use is relatively predictable, though this was not the case during the COVID pandemic, when manufacturers like Rolls-Royce lost a lot of money because the planes were not flying. Arrangements like the UK private finance initiative (PFI), where the defence department pays for a service like training or air-to-air refuelling, can only work effectively when the demand for the service is relatively predictable and the service is likely to be needed throughout the length of the contract. PFI is discussed further in Section 4.

3.1 Cost Growth Between Generations

Over time the growth in real unit production costs, after allowing for general inflation, between generations of a particular type of weapons system, such as fighter aircraft, has been growing rapidly. In Augustine (1987), the former head of Martin Marietta made the famous prediction, 'In the year 2054, the entire defence budget will purchase just one aircraft. The aircraft will have to be shared by the Air Force and navy, 3.5 days each week except for leap year, when it will be made available for the Marines for the extra day.' There are many estimates of this underlying growth. Kirkpatrick (2004) gives a figure for unit production cost growth on tactical combat aircraft of 10 per cent a year in real terms (removing the effect of general inflation). The consequence of this cost growth is that each new generation of tank, aircraft or ship costs a lot more than the unit it replaces.

Part of this cost growth is not pure inflation but reflects performance enhancement and improved capability; separating cost changes into their price and performance elements is difficult, though Bongers and Torres (2014) try. They provide a measure of technological change in US jet fighter aircraft from 1944 using hedonic regression, which makes the price of an aircraft a function of the performance and technological characteristics of the aircraft. This is a parametric model where the variables used to explain price are thrust, climb rate, maximum take-off weight, whether it had advanced avionics and whether it had stealth characteristics. Although the flyaway cost of a jet fighter, not corrected for inflation, has risen on average by 12.63 per cent a year, their quality-adjusted cost measure has risen by about 2.6 per cent a year. This is lower than the rate of inflation over this period of around 4 per cent per year. But it is cost, not quality-adjusted cost, that has to come out of the budget. That 10 per cent growth in quality has to be paid for.

The growth in average cost between generations reflects a set of vicious circles, or positive feedback loops, driving up costs. There tend to be diminishing returns to technology, so that adding an extra 5 per cent to performance may add 50 per cent to the cost of a system. But the effectiveness of a military system does not depend on its absolute technical performance but on its performance relative to an enemy. Because it is relative performance that matters in combat, countries are in the position of the Red Queen in Lewis Carroll's *Through the Looking-Glass*: 'It takes all the running you can do to stay in the same place'. This Red Queen effect is important in evolution, which is also driven by relative fitness. It is described by the economic theory of tournaments, where only winning counts. Kirkpatrick (2004) examines the various vicious circles that generate this cost escalation between generations. Quality has to be improved to match the threat and this makes the equipment more expensive.

Since costs between generations grow faster than the budget, one can only afford smaller numbers of units in each generation. This reduction in numbers means that fixed costs are spread over a smaller number and the benefits of economies of scale and learning curves are lost, raising the unit production costs. Learning curves come from the experience gained in production, causing costs to fall with the total number of units produced. Economies of scale depend on the rate of production, the number produced in any period of time. There also appears to be a tendency for fixed costs, such as software and networks to support the system, to grow relative to variable costs, the production cost of each unit.

Rising costs increase the temptation to keep the systems longer, making the gaps between generations longer. The longer gap means skills are lost and a bigger technological leap is required between generations, both making it more expensive. As noted earlier, many military platforms, like the US B-52 bombers, are very old. The capability of the platform is maintained by updates and the insertion of new avionics, electronics, sensors and weapons. The vicious circles interact. Technological competition for relative performance causes cost escalation, which causes smaller numbers to be produced with longer gaps between generations, further increasing the cost escalation, reducing the number acquired, and so on.

3.2 Cost Growth on Projects

Weapons typically cost a lot more than initially estimated. To a certain extent these forecast failures reflect the 'conspiracy of optimism' by which the military and industry have incentives to under-estimate costs to get the project accepted and included in the planned budget. There will be changes in specification which add to costs. Quantities are reduced and production rates slowed because of budget constraints. These increase unit costs, because of the large fixed costs. Fox (2011, p. 7) reports that the F–22 was originally expected to cost \$88 billion in 2009 for 648 aircraft. In March 2009, the programme was estimated to cost \$73.7 billion for the much smaller quantity of 184 aircraft. If there is a cost-plus contract, the firm has no incentives to reduce costs. The impact of contracting on costs is discussed in detail in Section 5.

On long projects, the agreed initial price is often indexed to allow for inflation: the agreed price is increased each year in line with some price index. This is sensible and provides insurance for the contractor. However, there are many possible indexes and one needs to choose between them.

The contractor for the UK EH101 helicopter, IBM, suggested one index; the MoD insisted on another index. The National Audit Office (NAO 1993) concluded that the MoD would have saved £70 million if they had accepted the index IBM suggested. This got very little publicity or political attention at the time the NAO reported, probably because politicians and journalists find discussion of price indexes very boring. The difference between the indexes was that the one suggested by IBM was a price index and the one the MoD insisted on was a cost index. Costs tend to grow faster than prices so more would be paid to the contractor using a cost index than a price index.

Productivity growth means that even if input costs, such as labour and material, are growing, improved efficiency means that the items can be produced for less. Thus, for general indexes, the growth in prices is less than the growth in costs. For the UK on average this difference was about 2 per cent a year until about 2010, when, for unknown reasons, aggregate productivity stopped growing. Productivity growth differs between sectors and is much faster in areas such as electronics. For many firms, despite high inflation in input costs like wages and raw materials, they are selling higher quality goods at lower prices because of technological progress and productivity growth. Whether there is productivity growth in defence production is difficult to judge because one needs a measure of defence output to measure productivity.

Cost estimation is often seen as making a central forecast. Clients want one number, not three. The US President Lyndon Baines Johnson asked one of his economists what unemployment next year would be. The economist answered, 'In the range 6–8%.' LBJ, a Texan, responded, 'Ranges are for cattle, give me a number.' The problems with central forecasts in economics are explained in Castle et al. (2019). However, the estimation process must assess the various risks, make allowance for those risks and include contingencies for them in the budget. RAND Europe (2021) classifies risks under four main headings. Technical risk is the danger that the development of critical technologies does not meet the programme objectives in terms of cost, time and performance. Design risk is the danger that the weapons system's design will not result in effective operation or be easy to produce. System integration risk is the danger that new and existing technologies employed in the weapons system do not work together and/or interact properly. Business risk is the danger that the procedures to select the contractor and contract design do not lead to effective project delivery. In practice, there is too little allowance for risk and the cost estimates approved at the main investment decision point can often exceed the worst-case scenario modelled at the point of initial approval.

3.3 Cost Growth on the Budget

In the national accounts, aggregates such as GDP are expressed in both current and constant (adjusted for inflation) prices. The constant price measure gives an estimate of the real output of the economy. The ratio of GDP at current prices to GDP at constant prices is a price index called the GDP deflator. This is probably the most general price index for a country but there is a large number of other price indexes which measure prices in different sectors of the economy. The Consumer Price Indexes, which is a measure of the cost of living, is probably the most familiar since it is widely used for many purposes, including as an inflation target for the Bank of England. Inflation is the percentage change in the price index. This raises the issue as to how we should measure military prices, or defence inflation, to get an estimate of the real output of the military sector.

To measure prices you need a measure of the quantity of output. For goods, output is measured by the number of units produced. For services – such as banking, education or health – measuring output is more difficult, but possible. It is not clear how one would measure defence output. An unsuccessful attempt was made in the UK to construct a measure of defence output to match existing output figures for health and education spending.

It is quite common to measure defence inflation from the input side, with an implicit assumption that productivity growth is zero. Some input costs are reasonably easy to measure. Wages tend to grow at the same rate as the economy as a whole. Fuel prices tend to move with oil prices. Defence benefits from being an intensive user of the inputs whose prices have fallen most rapidly: electronic and IT equipment. In the USA, defence prices indexes are largely input-based. The UK also calculated an input-based measure of defence inflation. But after a consultation in 2017, publication was stopped. It was not clear for what purposes it was useful.

3.4 Concluding Comments

The factors influencing cost growth in defence are very different for each type of cost growth: between generations, on projects and on the budget as a whole. There are major technical problems in measuring each of these types of cost growth, primarily because there is no unambiguous measure of the quantity of defence output. Between-generation cost growth measures can allow for quantifiable performance characteristics, like the speed or payload of an aircraft, but they may not be the important factors for performance in combat. Within-project cost growth can compare final costs with initial estimates, but that does not indicate whether the final price represented good value for money. It might have cost many times the initial estimate but still provide effective defence, were it possible to measure effective defence. Measures of overall defence inflation are desired in order to deflate expenditure to get a measure of real defence output. But if one cannot measure output, one cannot measure inflation. The Public Accounts Committee (PAC 2021a, p. 9) reported, 'When asked if the financial problems with the Defence budget were ever likely to change, the Permanent Secretary pointed first to the Department not having a very good understanding of the drivers of inflation with defence projects.'

Just as postponing equipment replacement to save money in the short run adds to long-run costs, postponing repairs to the roof is likely to make the eventual cost higher, as a consequence of both the damage done by leaks and the more extensive repairs required. There is the difference that, while a country may decide to manage without the capability and not replace the equipment, a household is unlikely to choose to do without a roof.

4 Sources: Where to Buy the Weapons?

The sources of the weapon can be described either in terms of the location of development and production or in terms of the type of organisation that provides them. In terms of location, a defence department can acquire military equipment by: (a) importing something developed and produced in another country, (b) producing it domestically under licence from a design developed elsewhere, (c) designing and producing it in collaboration with other countries, or (d) designing and producing it domestically. Importing tends to be the cheapest, followed by licensed production and collaboration. Domestic development and production is usually the most expensive. These categories fade into each other. In the 1960s, after cancelling the TSR-2 aircraft, the UK acquired the US F-4 Phantom. To maintain industry employment and skills it installed larger Rolls-Royce engines. This involved major changes to the plane and a large increase in cost relative to an 'off-the-shelf' purchase of a standard F-4. In the 1980s, the UK licensed production of the Brazilian Tucano trainer, by Short Brothers of Belfast. But it was said that at the end of all the modifications made by the RAF, all that remained of the original aircraft was the name.

Uttley and Wilkinson (2019) argue that at the heart of defence procurement lies a great paradox. It is the tension a state feels between the need for sovereignty, the imperative to secure the supply of defence equipment, and the need for integration, the imperative to share the enormous costs of defence production with other states. In interaction, the supply-side and demand-side forces conflict. On the supply side, the increasing returns to scale mean that the industry should be global with very few players. On the demand side, the preference for domestic production means that government support enables more players to survive. There are two producers of large commercial airliners but more than a dozen producers of fast jet combat aircraft. In principle collaboration with other friendly countries maintains a degree of sovereignty and shares costs but in practice it faces great difficulties.

In terms of organisation, weapons may be provided from: a government-owned operation, such as an arsenal or state-owned company; a government-owned contractor-operated (GOCO) facility like AWE, discussed earlier; or a private company. The purchase may be customised, specifically developed for the buyer, or purchased as either commercial off-the-shelf (COTS) or military off-the-shelf (MOTS).

There are hybrid forms of organisation such as the UK public–private partnerships (PPP) and PFI, a form of PPP, described in Ansari (2019), which have been copied elsewhere. Despite having pioneered them, the UK government announced in 2018 that it would no longer use PFIs, after some bad experiences. Under a PFI, rather than purchasing the equipment and maintaining it in-house, the defence department enters a long-term, perhaps twenty-five-year, contract with a consortium of companies to purchase particular services like pilot training or air-to-air refuelling. Through a special purpose vehicle (SPV) created for the purpose, the consortium borrows the money to develop and construct the facilities and equipment, which it leases to the defence department. Having developed the system, the consortium should have the required operational expertise and an incentive to build in reliability, since it is only paid when it provides the service. When the facilities are not needed by the defence department, the consortium can use them for other purposes. Air-to-air refuelling tankers are used for freight, for instance. This reduces the cost to the defence department.

The consortium pays a higher interest rate than the government, but the borrowing does not appear as government debt. It is off-balance-sheet, which may be a political advantage. At the early stages of a PFI, before the facilities have been built, there is considerable risk attached to the enterprise and interest rates are high. When the facilities are completed, the risk is much lower and the revenue streams for the services are guaranteed. The SPV can then refinance at a lower interest rate, increasing its profits considerably. PFIs enable the defence department to acquire equipment that it could not otherwise afford. Rather than paying to buy the equipment now at full cost, it commits itself to a stream of future payments. This may be at a higher total cost and those services may not be needed if the security situation changes. Premature ending of a PFI because of changed circumstances can be expensive as the consortium has to be compensated for the cancelled contract.

After a discussion of the policy issues and industrial structure in terms of monopoly and concentration, this section examines the international dimension of arms procurement.

4.1 Defence Industrial and Technology Policy

Maintenance of a defence industrial and technological base is a central objective of any defence department. In the USA, it is the responsibility of the Deputy Assistant Secretary of Defense for Industrial Policy. Dunne et al. (2007) provide an economic model of the process. Determining the appropriate defence industrial base that can supply current, future and emergency military requirements is difficult. The ministry must decide: the number of different types of systems required and the quality and quantity of each; the extent to which it can trust allies to collaborate in production or to provide imports, especially during a conflict; the potential export market for the systems; the degree to which exports are taxed or subsidised; and the security consequences of those exports. All these judgements have to be made subject to a budget constraint. The need for a technology base was discussed in Section 2.

The policy instruments available include: structuring procurement competitions to determine the number of players; funding R&D to encourage innovation and entrants; regulating mergers; allocating industrial resources; controlling arms exports; and controlling investment by foreign firms. State ownership of arms firms extends the instruments. When the government is the only domestic buyer for a system its procurement determines national industrial structure by default. In practice, determining what is wanted is complicated by industrial issues, political accountability, budgetary uncertainty, inter-operability with other countries, compatibility between different systems and compliance with complex regulations. Few governments feel that these issues can be left to market forces. Transparency may be an issue; the government may not be aware of the existence of small specialist providers with unique skills and only discover them when they cease production. The Department of Defense (DOD 2022, p. 18) discusses castings and forgings, products that are critical to defence, but DOD business is unattractive because it orders in small quantities and has highly specialised requirements so some firms simply choose to exit the market, losing specialist skills and tacit knowledge that is difficult to replace.

The maintenance of skills in the domestic industry requires a steady flow of orders. But the flow required to maintain an industrial capability may not match the flow required to maintain the defence capability. The gap between orders for generations of UK nuclear submarines resulted in a loss of skills and the problems with the Astute class discussed in Section 5. Taylor (2022), discussing the lessons of Ajax, concluded that the failure in armoured vehicles underlined the necessity for government to maintain a drumbeat of orders if it wishes to maintain a national industrial capability in a sector.

In the UK, NAO (2021) noted that the MoD has programmes with a total budgeted whole-life cost of £162.6 billion in 2019–20 and relies on a limited specialist supplier base to meet its needs: 44 per cent of its £26.6 billion procurement expenditure went to ten major providers, nine of which are involved directly in the supply of military equipment: Airbus, Babcock, BAE, General Dynamics, Leonardo, Lockheed Martin, QinetiQ, Rolls-Royce and Boeing.

While the major providers are now private companies, in 1979 much of the British arms industry was state-owned, including four of the seven firms paid over £100 million a year by the MoD. Royal Ordnance factories had always been state-owned. British Aerospace and British Shipbuilders were formed when Labour nationalised aircraft and shipbuilding companies in 1977. Rolls-Royce was nationalised in 1971 by the Conservatives after being bankrupted by the development of the RB211 civil engine. Subsequently, the Conservatives under Margaret Thatcher privatised all the arms firms and introduced competition under Peter Levene, the head of defence procurement during the 1980s. The commitment to competition was given credibility by the occasional cancellation of the domestic project and a foreign purchase, such as replacing Nimrod AEW with the Boeing Sentry AWACS in 1986. This reliance on competition and markets meant that the UK did not have an explicit defence industrial policy from 1979 until 2002, when Labour developed the 2005 Defence Industrial Strategy and a subsequent Defence Technology Strategy. The coherence and feasibility of these strategies were widely questioned because the budget available was not large enough to support the industrial aspirations. As noted above, in 2021 the Conservatives renationalised AWE and nationalised Sheffield Forgemaster, a supplier of critical parts for UK nuclear submarines.

In France the relationship between the state and the military sector was different, reflecting their different industrial traditions: French dirigisme, British laissez-faire. In France a tight symbiotic relationship existed between the procurement agency, the Direction Générale de l'Armement (DGA), and what were originally largely nationalised arms firms. There has been some privatisation but the state still retains a considerable shareholding in many arms companies. French military-industrial politics can be quite complex. The negotiations between the French state, which has a 26 per cent shareholding in Thales, and Dassault, which has a 25 per cent shareholding, can be convoluted.

Despite the close relationship between the French state and the arms firms, there has been less restructuring and globalisation of the arms industry in France than in the UK. While the DGA has encouraged consolidation and rationalisation, progress has been slow. France and the UK are further compared in Section 6. Ownership does not imply control. State ownership can mean that the arms industry can control the state rather than the state controlling the arms industry. The state may have more control when the firms are private, since it can use its great leverage as the sole buyer of weapons without responsibility.

4.2 Monopoly and Competition

Domestic monopoly is common in weapons supply because of economies of scale. The power of a monopolist is reduced if it is facing a single buyer, a monopsonist, as is usual in defence. The relative bargaining strength of monopolist and monopsonist will depend on factors such as the cost to each of not coming to an agreement. If there is only a single supplier, a competitive fixed-price contract will not work: the monopolists, with private information about its costs, can bid high and still get the contract. Economists call this an information rent. With cost-plus, the monopolist has to reveal their costs, though monitoring true costs may be difficult. Even where there are foreign competitors, a single national supplier may gain great leverage from the political unacceptability of buying abroad. Even if there is potential competition before the contract, once one firm wins a contract, it gains some monopoly power. The contract winner gets the intellectual property rights (IPR) and tacit knowledge necessary to complete the contract, making it difficult and expensive to replace the incumbent.

While economies of scale and scope and learning curves make a single supplier look cheaper, competition can force down prices. This trade-off is difficult to quantify. Pratt and Whitney was the sole supplier of engines for the F-15 and F-16, but after poor performance in 1984 the DOD introduced General Electric as a second source. The main engine supplier for the F-35 is also Pratt and Whitney. The General Electric engine being developed as an alternative was cancelled in 2011 owing to lack of funding. Of course, the threat of a potential second source may stop Pratt and Whitney trying to exploit its position.

In 1993, a US merger wave was stimulated by the 'last supper' when Pentagon Deputy Secretary Perry told a dinner of defence industry executives that they were expected to start merging. There was a major consolidation of the industry which ended when the Pentagon decided that it had gone far enough and blocked the merger of Lockheed Martin with Northrop Grumman in early 1997. The Department of Defense (DOD 2022, p. 5) gives data on the number of US-based prime contractors in various weapons categories. Between 1990 and

1998 the number of contractors dropped from thirteen to three in tactical missiles and from eight to three in fixed-wing aircraft. It was still three in both cases in 2020. It also discusses more general issues associated with competition in the defence industry in the United States.

The merger wave after the end of the Cold War was not confined to the USA. The European Airbus (EADS) and MBDA, the missile consortium, expanded by merger and acquisition. The French company Thompson CSF acquired a range of defence companies, including the UK company Racal, rebranding itself Thales. The Italian company Finmeccanica also acquired a range of defence companies, including the UK Westland helicopter business, and rebranded itself Leonardo.

Carril and Duggan (2020) study the relationship between market structure and public procurement outcomes. In particular, they ask whether and to what extent the consolidation-driven increases in the US defence industry concentration affect the way in which the government procures its goods and services. The US defence mergers during the 1990s caused the share of contract dollars awarded to the five largest DOD contractors to rise from 21.7 per cent in 1990 to 31.3 per cent in 2000. Using detailed data on DOD contracts, they find that increased concentration caused the procurement process to become less competitive, with an increase in the share of spending awarded without competition or via single-bid solicitations, and induced a shift from fixed-price to cost-plus contracts. However, they found no evidence that consolidation led to a significant increase in acquisition costs because DOD buyer power stopped the firms from exercising any additional market power gained by consolidation

4.3 Internationalisation

During the Cold War, countries were seen as being on an industrial ladder of weapons production capacity. On the top rung were countries like the United States and the Soviet Union, largely self-sufficient. On the next rung down were countries like the UK and France with large defence industries but needing to import some elements. On lower rungs were countries with capacities in some areas then at the bottom of the ladder were those with minimal arms production capability. However, internationalisation of the defence supply chain makes the idea of national production capabilities less relevant and changing technology means that countries cannot be neatly placed on a ladder. Cheap Turkish drones have played a major role in recent conflicts, such as those in Libya and between Armenia and Azerbaijan.

There are many aspects to internationalisation. It may refer to the construction of a transnational company like Airbus, to a US company owning subsidiaries that produce in many countries or to the structure of the supply chain. The inputs into something produced in the USA by a US company can come from all over the world. An F-16 aircraft, apparently of US origin, will contain components from all over the world and may have been assembled in Taiwan, Turkey or South Korea. Braddon (2019) discusses the evolution of the defence supply chain. There is also increasing concern about the resilience of the commercial supply chain in the face of shocks like the COVID pandemic. For instance, automobile manufacturers had to restrict production because they were not able to source semi-conductors. Firms started to maintain increased inventories and moved from 'just in time' to 'just in case'.

The Stockholm International Peace Research Institute (SIPRI 2021) reports that the fifteen largest arms companies have headquarters in eight countries, but foreign entities in forty-nine different countries. A foreign entity is a branch, subsidiary or joint venture that is registered in a country other than the one in which the company has its headquarters. On the SIPRI definition, Thales is the most internationalised with sixty-seven entities registered in twenty-four countries, though the company says it operates in over fifty countries. Airbus has forty-one in twenty-four countries; Leonardo fifty-nine in twenty-one countries; Boeing fifty-six in twenty-one countries; Lockheed Martin twenty-eight in nineteen countries. Many of these entities were involved in manufacturing, primarily in North America, Europe and Australia. SIPRI notes that the market has become increasingly competitive and discusses the factors that prompt internationalisation by mergers, acquisitions and joint ventures. The factors include gaining economies of scale, pooling risks, diversifying their portfolios and pressures from buying governments for local production. US restrictions on arms imports and the size of the US market mean that there are many foreign entities located in the United States.

Nationality may not match markets. Although BAE is nominally a British company, the USA accounted for 43 per cent of its total sales in the 2019 financial year and in the past has accounted for over half. What is treated as national differs between countries. The USA insists on production being in the USA and restricts the role of non-US citizens in the subsidiary. The UK tends to care about the production being in the UK; the French tend to care about ownership. Oudot and Bellais (2019) discuss globalisation in the context of the French defence industry.

The UK openness to foreign acquisition has become controversial. In 2019 a US private equity company, Advent International, bought a UK defence contractor, Cobham, then broke it up, selling half by value, within 18 months. The guarantees given to the MoD were not transferred to the buyers. By 2021 Cobham had no UK manufacturing facilities but tried to buy another defence company, Ultra Electronics. This was referred to the Competition and Markets Authority by the business secretary on national security grounds. In August 2021 TransDigm tried to buy Meggitt, in the face of an agreed bid by Parker Hannifin, another US company, and then pulled out of the race. The business secretary asked for assurances about military supply from Parker Hannifin.

TransDigm acquired US specialist defence companies with monopoly power; over 75 per cent of its sales came from products where it was the sole supplier. After acquiring a company it raised prices sharply. In 2019 the DOD accused it of price gouging – seventeen of its products had margins of more than 1000 per cent – and it repaid $16 million. A similar practice, acquiring companies that are the only source of a drug and sharply raising prices, has also been followed in US pharmaceutical markets. If the market is small or the costs of entry are high, potential competitors know that the incumbent can cut prices as soon as the challenger has incurred the cost of entry, making entry unprofitable. Buyer power is more effective than competition in such situations. In the USA, upsetting patients who need a drug has less serious consequences than upsetting the Pentagon.

Chinese and Russian firms have become increasingly important in the process of internationalisation. Historically China was Russia's largest arms market but Russian exports to China have been falling since the early 2000s, as China built up its production capability. Chinese arms production is dominated by a small number of state-owned defence conglomerates that also produce civilian goods. Many are said to lack the dynamism of the Chinese private sector, being portrayed as lumbering and inefficient monopolists. Against this there is a long-standing policy of 'Military Civilian Fusion' and dynamic companies like Huawei have a history of linkages to the People's Liberation Army. The Chinese emphasis on low-cost mass production of weapons gives it an edge in the parts of the international market where cost is more important than performance. There are some areas where China has demonstrated very advanced technology, including in November 2021 being able to fire a separate missile from a hypersonic missile.

4.4 The Arms Trade

Because of concerns with security of supply in conflict, governments desire to foster a defence industrial base and fear that importing will make them dependent on a foreign seller, who may not be willing to resupply in time of conflict or may charge high prices for spares and munitions once the buyer is locked in. But despite the preference for self-sufficiency, the vast cost of domestic development and production of major weapons systems means that countries often have no choice but to import, so a trade in arms develops. Because so many countries subsidise their arms industry to maintain a defence industrial base and want to spread the costs by selling abroad, the arms export market is very competitive. The firms make money – they would not sell otherwise – but it is not clear that there is an economic benefit to the country from exporting arms. Chalmers et al. (2002) review the evidence for an economic benefit to the UK of arms exports.

The Stockholm International Peace Research Institute (SIPRI 2021) estimates that the trade in major weapons systems is less than half a per cent of total world trade. The top ten exporters in 2016–20 were the United States, Russia, France, Germany, China, UK, Spain, Israel, South Korea, Italy. Exporting is more concentrated than importing. Whereas the top five exporters account for 76 per cent of total exports, the top five importers only account for 36 per cent of total imports. The top ten importers in the same period were Saudi Arabia, India, Egypt, Australia, China, Algeria, South Korea, Qatar, UAE, Pakistan. There are a few large producer countries and the remainder import nearly all their major weapons systems. Even the largest producer, the United States, has to import some systems. For instance, the USA has used UK short take-off vertical landing technology in the AV8B, a Harrier derivative used by the Marines, and in the F-35. So the USA is both the largest exporter and the thirteenth largest importer, down from the ninth largest in 2011–15. These numbers are based on SIPRI trend indicator values; SIPRI also gives some national estimates of the financial value based on orders, licences or deliveries. Orders may be cancelled and payments may not be made. The trade in major weapons systems, where the transfer is usually apparent, is rather different from the trade in small arms and light weapons (SALW), where illicit transactions are common.

While the arms trade has economic aspects, it is always geopolitical. Turkey is a member of NATO but antagonistic to another member, Greece. Turkish Aerospace Industry produces F-16s under licence from the United States and has plans for an indigenous fighter aircraft. However, the Turkish purchase of the S-400 Russian air defence system led the USA to remove Turkey from the F-35 programme in 2019, stopping Turkey taking delivery of over 100 F-35s. In October 2021 Turkey tried to persuade the USA to upgrade its F-16s. Geopolitics played a role in the 2021 decision by Australia to cancel its order for French conventional submarines and instead acquire nuclear submarines as part of the AUKUS trilateral agreement with the USA and UK, provoking strong reactions from both France and China.

French foreign policy has often been driven by the desire to export arms. Equipment design has often reflected perceived foreign demand rather than French military needs, prompting complaints by the armed services. Coulomb and Fontanel (2005) comment that French arms exports were sometimes promoted without any economic or commercial logic, particularly when firms tried to compensate for domestic budget cuts by increasing exports. France lost $1.2 billion on the $3.4 billion 1993 order for 436 Leclerc tanks for the UAE, mainly from problems with foreign exchange hedging. In 2003 the French government ordered the arms firms not to offer products below production price. The choice in February 2012 by India to purchase 126 Rafale aircraft was said to be on the basis of a low whole-life cost. There was then considerable controversy in India and allegations of corruption and price escalation. A large number of different prices were quoted and there was considerable confusion about what was included in each of the prices. The contract was reduced to thirty-six aircraft on different terms and delivery began in 2020. British foreign policy has also been driven by arms exports on occasion, for example the Al Yamamah programme of arms exports to Saudi Arabia. The contract, initially signed in 1985, was worth about £40 billion over its first two decades and is still continuing today as Project Salam.

Prices for arms transfers are complicated because contracts for the sale of major weapons systems involve not just the platform and munitions but also spares, training, maintenance and sometimes operating the equipment, which can be more profitable than the main sale. In 2008, the value of the initial order of seventy-two UK Typhoons by Saudi Arabia was put at £4.3 billion; armaments and weapons systems added £5 billion, and maintenance training and support added another £10 billion. This sale required US approval because the aircraft contained US technology.

Financing may involve 'countertrade', barter, payment in commodities. Saudi Arabia paid for the Tornados bought under Al Yamamah in oil. The sales are often financed through export credits, provided by the country of the supplying firm, and may involve offsets, promises by the supplier to locate production in the buying country. Matthews (2019b) provides a survey of offsets, which are often intended to improve the technological or productive capacity of the buyer. Suppliers typically charge a premium to cover the extra cost of offset. Lack of transparency about arms trade contracts makes it difficult to estimate how large the premium is.

Technological spin-offs from military development to commercial products do not seem to be an important source of competitive advantage, though there are exceptions. Conversion from military production to civilian production is often hazardous since different skills are required in the two markets. For instance, technological advance is given much greater weight than cost-minimisation in military markets, in contrast to civilian markets. Matthews (2019b, p. 164) concludes: 'Customer governments clearly hold a positive view on the worth of offset, otherwise demand for it would disappear. This perspective is surprising as the evidence, to date, does not support the view that offset has had a material impact on industrial and technological development.'

Bidding for arms export contracts can be an expensive business: setting up subsidiaries in the buying country, demonstrating the technology, providing specialist advice and entering competitions. This investment is wasted if the contract is not obtained. Even when there are potential export markets, government regulation may stop companies meeting the demand through arms embargoes and controls. Selling arms requires a range of specialist skills, particularly the ability to influence the buying government, which may require bribes and other corrupt tactics. The deals are rarely transparent and there can be disputes about the quality of the items purchased. Secrecy, the unique nature and complexity of each contract and the uncertainty about quality provide scope for corruption and fraud. Feinstein (2011) gives a range of examples. Corruption is not peculiar to arms exports; similar factors make it common in the construction industry. BAE suffered reputation effects over the alleged bribery associated with the Al Yamamah sales to Saudi Arabia. Since the contract was between the UK and Saudi governments, and both governments seem to have been aware of the payments, it is not clear that the company, as distinct from the governments concerned, was responsible for the corruption. The corruption associated with the large South African arms deal, the Strategic Defence Package, has played a major role in the politics of that country.

4.5 Export Controls

Governments both promote and control arms exports and each country has its own export control regime. Exports of weapons and dual-use equipment, which can have both military and civilian applications, raise major security concerns. Countries do not want to arm their enemies or have their allies arm them, thus co-ordination is useful. States may also wish to avoid supplying arms that might worsen an existing conflict, contribute to a destabilising arms race or be used in violation of human rights and international humanitarian law. National export controls typically involve: lists of products that require a licence; lists of countries to which exports can or cannot be made; customs procedures to stop unlicensed exports and some system to specify the end-use of the equipment to stop it being re-exported. Controls may be evaded through purchase by a country not subject to restrictions who tranships the weapons to a restricted country. This can be a particular problem with components and subsystems. If country A makes subsystems for a weapons system produced in country B, with different export control criteria, then B may sell the weapons to a country which A would not itself supply. Often A can do little about it because it has little leverage over B. But when A is America, it has the power, which it uses, to restrict re-export, stopping B exporting weapons with US-made subsystems. In these circumstances B has an incentive not to use US components that might be subject to restriction.

Supplies are also restricted by UN embargoes, of which there were thirteen in 2020, and the Arms Trade Treaty (ATT), though there are varying levels of compliance with both. The 2013 ATT entered into force in December 2014. At the end of 2021, 110 states were party to the treaty. A further thirty-one had signed but not ratified, including the USA where President Trump threatened to withdraw from the ATT. The treaty attempts to establish common standards that must be met before states authorise weapons transfers, reduce the illicit arms trade and promote accountability and transparency by state-parties concerning transfers of conventional arms. Implementation is a matter for the individual signatories so varies considerably. Over the years the level of reporting has declined.

There are four multilateral export control regimes by which potential suppliers co-ordinate their actions: the Australia group for chemical and biological weapons, the missile technology control regime, the nuclear suppliers group and the Wassenaar Arrangement for conventional arms and dual-use items and technologies. These are informal groups that co-ordinate trade controls and related policies. They are described in SIPRI (2021).

European states are major suppliers of military equipment and competitors in export markets. But given their different economic and security interests, a sale that seems problematic to one may not seem problematic to another. Disagreements about supply to actors in the Syrian Civil War and to Saudi Arabia of equipment used in the Yemeni Civil War are examples. In an attempt to avoid this problem, the EU in 2008 defined common rules governing control of exports of military technology and equipment which replaced an earlier Code of Conduct on arms exports. This Common Position contains eight risk assessment criteria and transparency measures that all EU countries apply to their licensing decisions for exports of conventional weapons on the 'EU Common Military List'. There are also regulations covering the export, re-export, brokering and transit of dual-use goods, software and technology.

To reduce the danger of countries thinking, 'If I don't supply, someone else will', no undercutting conventions can be used. If one supplier refuses to supply, it informs the others, who should not supply either. Within the EU system, member states have to circulate through diplomatic channels details of licences refused, with an explanation of why the licence has been refused. Before any member state grants a licence which has been denied by another member state for an essentially identical transaction within the last three years, it has firstly to consult the state or states that issued the denial. If, after consultations, the state nevertheless decides to grant a licence, it has to notify the state issuing the denial, giving a detailed explanation of its reasoning.

The Common Position is presently the sole example of a group of states that have agreed to co-ordinate conventional arms exports with a supranational constraining mechanism. The UK played a central role in this process, for instance drafting the control list, thus the UK's exit from the EU had implications for this system. There were twenty-one EU embargoes in force during 2020, eight of which had no UN counterpart, including China. Again there are varying levels of compliance because EU members implement it through their own export control systems and have considerable freedom to determine what is covered. Differing attitudes to export control among EU states have caused difficulties in collaborative projects, Germany having stricter rules than others.

Countries differ on what constitutes the legitimate security needs of a potential customer state. Who is thought to be a safe customer can change. During the 1991 Gulf War after the Iraqi invasion of Kuwait, French Mirages had to be withdrawn from the conflict because they were indistinguishable on radar from the Mirages France sold to Iraq. Effective embargoes or controls can be counterproductive if they provide strong incentives to develop a domestic arms industry and acquire weapons of mass destruction in the target state. This was the case with Apartheid South Africa and currently North Korea and Iran.

4.6 The Structure of the Global Defence Industry

One widely used measure of the structure of an industry is the degree of concentration, measured by the share of the largest firms: the smaller the share of the top firms, the more competitive the industry is thought to be. While at a national level there may be domestic monopolies, at a global level the arms industry is not very concentrated. Using the SIPRI data on the top 100 arms-producing companies, the market share of the top five firms went up from 22 per cent in 1990 to a peak of 45 per cent in 2002 in a wave of post–Cold War mergers and exits. The share of the top five then fell to a low of 33 per cent in 2014, staying around 35 per cent to 2018. SIPRI changed the format of the data from 2019, but it seems to have been stable in 2019.

The SIPRI *Yearbook* (2021, table 9.7) lists the top twenty-five arms-producing and military services companies in 2019. The top five companies were all from the USA: Lockheed Martin, Boeing, Northrop Grumman, Raytheon and General Dynamics. Chinese companies were sixth, eighth and ninth (AVIC, CETC and NORINCO), though SIPRI emphasise that information on the Chinese companies is scarce and they have only recently been added to the list. The UK company BAE was seventh, US companies were tenth and eleventh – L3 Harris and United Technologies, respectively. The next three were European: Leonardo (Italy), Airbus (trans-European) and Thales (France). Number fifteen was Russian, Almaz-Antey; sixteen US, Huntington; seventeen French, Dassault. Numbers eighteen to twenty-one were from the USA: Honeywell, Leidos, Booz Allen Hamilton, General Electric. Number twenty-two was from the UAE: EDGE, created from a merger of twenty-five smaller firms. Number twenty-three was from the UK, Rolls-Royce; number twenty-four, CSGC China; number twenty-five, United Shipbuilding Russia. Some of the figures are estimates with a high degree of uncertainty. US companies accounted for 61 per cent of the total revenue, European companies 18 per cent, Chinese 16 per cent. Most of the top twenty-five companies were specialist arms producers. For ten companies, arms sales were over 80 per cent of total sales; for seven, between 40 and 80 per cent; and for eight, below 40 per cent.

From a commercial point of view the arms industry is not a particularly attractive market for large, legitimate western commercial firms and their share prices and profits tend to reflect this, being very volatile. The eventful history of BAE since privatisation, where bankruptcy loomed on more than one occasion, is an example. The large producers depend on purchases by their own government and changes in government policies and personnel can have an adverse impact on sales. The large firms that produce major weapons systems sold legitimately are located in relatively few countries. There is a large, less legitimate market for SALW. Production for this market is dispersed over many more countries and there is a rather different industrial structure.

Wars, and the consequent increase in demand for armaments, boost profits but survival in the slumps can be difficult. The Brazilian arms industry profited from the Iran–Iraq war but then demand collapsed. One Brazilian company, Embraer, produced the Tucano, a successful turboprop small aircraft used for military training, counter-insurgency and light attack, that was widely exported. It then moved away from the military market and managed to establish a dominant position, along with Bombardier, in the market for smaller regional passenger aircraft.

The large US technology companies have traditionally been reluctant to deal with the Pentagon, partly because the bureaucracy involved in contracting increases costs. As a space example, NASA claimed that the $400 million cost of developing Elon Musk's SpaceX Falcon 9 rocket was a tenth of the likely cost of a rocket built under traditional government contracting. As a result SpaceX leapt ahead of United Launch Alliance, the joint venture of the big traditional military contractors, Boeing and Lockheed Martin.

Commercial suppliers, such as Microsoft, may be unwilling to provide the guarantees or information that the public sector contracts have traditionally required, such as access to source code. The Department of Defense (DOD 2022, p. 12) discusses a range of issues that result from the use of commercial items in military equipment. It also discusses the issues involved in the management of IPR. Governments may restrict access to foreigners by, for instance, 'black-boxing' code. This has been an issue between the USA and UK over the F-35. Availability of suppliers may vary over the cycle as contractors substitute between public and private work.

Dunne and Skons (2021) discuss how the large tech companies may be becoming less reluctant to take military contracts. The first large DOD cloud initiative was the JEDI (Joint Enterprise Defense Infrastructure) project, worth $10 billion over ten years. Its aim was to develop a comprehensive cloud enterprise system for overall DOD activities. Cloud computing was already a large commercial area dominated by Amazon Web Services (AWS) followed by Microsoft Azure, with Google a distant third. Amazon is a company used to dealing with complex logistics and large amounts of data and working with low margins, so it is a difficult company for a traditional defence producer, used to long development times, small orders and high margins, to compete against.

In October 2019 the DOD announced that the JEDI contract had been awarded to Microsoft. It was alleged that this reflected President Trump's animosity to Amazon boss Jeff Bezos, who owned the *Washington Post* which was critical of the President. There was then an extended legal process and in July 2021 the DOD cancelled JEDI altogether, to replace it with a multi-cloud project which would involve more than one prime contractor. The US firm AWS has been hired by GCHQ and the other UK intelligence agencies to provide cloud computing.

4.7 Collaboration

Collaboration promises great benefits. Fixed costs are shared between many buyers and longer production runs bring the benefits of learning curves and economies of scale. The use of common equipment between countries aids inter-operability, maintenance, training and logistics. However, compromise is often required to get agreement about specification, often resulting in multiple versions. Inefficient work-sharing arrangements, lack of centralised control and elaborate bureaucratic procedures slow decision-making and increase costs. Workshare is often determined according to *juste retour* where work is allocated proportionally to the amount purchased, rather than to the most efficient supplier. Allocation may be more efficient when it is internalised within a transnational firm like MBDA, the missile consortium, or Airbus. Magill (2021) gives MBDA as a good example of effective Anglo-French collaboration, in the development of anti-ship missiles. However, Airbus had major difficulties with the development of the A400 M aircraft, discussed below.

Hartley (2019) reviews the history of collaborations. He points out that collaboration has mainly been in aerospace projects, because of their high fixed costs relative to land and sea systems. There tends to be a small number of partner nations, to minimise transaction costs, and project-specific consortia rather than transnational consortia. Rising costs are forcing more collaboration in land and sea projects, such as the MRAV (multi-role armoured vehicle) discussed below.

The history of European aircraft collaboration is complex, with a fluid mix of partners, usually couples and triples, forming temporary liaisons, with the companies involved merging and changing their name. What follows is a very simplified version. The numbers built are rough but an important indication of the potential for economies of scale and learning curves.

In the 1960s the UK and France co-operated in the production of the Jaguar, used in a close air support and strike role, manufactured by SEPECAT (Société Européenne de Production de l'avion Ecole de Combat et d'Appui Tactique), a joint venture between Breguet, which subsequently merged with Dassault, and the British Aircraft Corporation, a precursor to BAE. Over 500 were built and it was in service with the British and French air forces until the 2000s and was still operating with the Indian air force in the 2020s.

After the Jaguar, France developed the Dassault Mirage as a national programme. This was widely exported, its use in combat by the Israeli air force contributing to its appeal, and almost 1,500 were built. The UK joined Germany and Italy to develop the variable geometry, multi-role combat aircraft, the Tornado. The multi-role was a compromise to deal with the very different requirements of the partners and there were three variants: IDS (interdiction/strike), ECR (electronic combat, reconnaissance) and ADV (air defence variant, an interceptor). Almost 1,000 were built by Panavia (a consortium of BAE), MBB of Germany (which became part of Airbus) and Aeritalia (which became part of Leonardo). The UK export of the Tornado to Saudi Arabia was complicated by the fact that Germany had more stringent export controls than the UK. Tornados were still operational in the 2020s.

Development of the follow-on to the Tornado, the Eurofighter Typhoon, started in the 1980s; it first flew in the 1990s and entered service in the 2000s. Development was delayed by the end of the Cold War, which raised questions about the need for an aircraft of this sort. Initially, France was a member of the consortium but left to develop the Dassault Rafale, of which about 250 have been built. Rafale has been exported to India and Qatar, with a number of other orders placed, including eighty aircraft to the United Arab Emirates.

Eurofighter was manufactured by the successors to the companies that built Tornado: Airbus, BAE and Leonardo. Over 500 have been built. Matthews and Al-Saadi (2021) discuss the problems associated with the complex organisation of its collaborative production. The left wing is produced by Italy's Leonardo and the right wing is produced by Spain's Airbus. Their Table 3 lists the flaws in Eurofighter's collaborative supply chain. These include different business models of the industrial partners; political interference, changing national requirements and divergent budget cycles; different attitudes to protection of IPR and commercial interests and managing overhead costs; and the difficulty of agreeing export policy and the outsourcing and offshoring arrangements with third parties. It is not clear what the next generation of combat aircraft will be, or even if there will be another generation of manned aircraft. France, Germany and Spain are planning a Future Combat Air System, but Airbus and Dassault have found co-operation difficult and Germany's tighter export controls may again be an issue.

In the USA, the F-35 Joint Strike Fighter is a collaborative project in two dimensions, inter-service and international. It is joint between the US Air Force, Navy and Marines, though each has a different variant: F-35A for the Air Force, F-35B for the Marines, with short take-off and vertical landing, and F-35 C for the Navy, for operation from carriers. Having a common airframe and engine for such different variants has been debated. Although it is a US project, a large number of countries are involved, including the United Kingdom, which is a Level 1 partner contributing 10 per cent to development costs and taking delivery of F-35B. Australia, Canada, Italy, Norway, Denmark, the Netherlands, Israel and Singapore are 'Security Cooperative Participants'. Turkey was a participant until it was excluded for taking delivery of a Russian air defence system. The problems with the F-35 were discussed in Section 1. The F-35 is manufactured in several locations. Lockheed Martin builds the aircraft's forward section in Fort Worth, Texas. Northrop Grumman builds the midsection in Palmdale, California and the tail is built by BAE Systems in the United Kingdom. Final assembly of these components takes place in Fort Worth. Final assembly and checkout facilities have also been established in Italy and

Japan. Rolls-Royce builds the lift system for the F-35B in the USA (CRS 2022, p. 29).

Airbus (previously EADS) produced the A400 M military transport aircraft for a group of countries, initially under a fixed-price contract. Airbus incurred about €2 billion in extra development costs, primarily because of problems with the propulsion system. The first flight at the end of 2009 was a year late and cancellation was possible because deliveries were three years behind schedule, costs had overrun and targets for carrying capacity had not been met. The contract was renegotiated and A400 M has been in service since 2015, though UK entry into service was six years late.

OCCAR, the Organisation for Joint Armament Cooperation, manages the A400 M programme. It is a European intergovernmental organisation that facilitates and manages collaborative armament programmes through their life cycle. It involves Belgium, France, Germany, Italy, Spain and the UK and managed sixteen procurement projects in late 2021. OCCAR also managed the collaborative MRAV project that produced Boxer. MRAV started in 1993 as a joint venture between France and Germany. The UK joined in 1996 and France left in 1999. The UK then left in 2003 because it wanted high protection in a light vehicle, less than 20 tons, transportable in a C-130 Hercules. Germany insisted that this was impossible and was proved right (Akam 2021, p. 648). Boxer entered service in Germany in 2009. The UK then tried to develop various vehicles but failed (HCDC 2021) and in 2019 ordered over 520 Boxers. Had it stayed in MRAV it could have had Boxer much earlier, which may have saved lives in Iraq and Afghanistan.

4.8 Concluding Comments

This section has looked at the range of different sources from which countries can obtain their weapons. Householders face the same problem finding a reliable builder. If they want the work done quickly, the builder who is immediately available is the one who does not have many customers, perhaps because they are not very good. This is adverse selection. The large firm, with a good reputation, is likely to be more expensive because it has higher overheads and its employees may be less motivated than the self-employed builder who needs the work. Which is best depends on things that the householder does not know, like the quality of the various builders. The householders can put the job out to tender: specify what needs to be done, contact lots of builders, ask each to bid for the job and choose the one that seems to offer the best value for money. The alternative is to get to know a builder, perhaps through recommendations, who will advise on what work needs to be done and invoice for work done as they go along. This choice is the subject of the next section.

5 Contracts: How to Buy the Weapons?

Weapons contracts have to cover a range of technical, commercial and legal contingencies, and comply with complex accounting systems. They are usually drawn up by specialist contracting officers who may have difficulty communicating with other stakeholders, who belong to different tribes with different languages. Many of these complications will be ignored for the moment to focus on the choice between broad types of economic contract and the principal-agent issues that surround these contracts.

5.1 Types of Contract

Consider a defence department's choice between a fixed-price contract awarded after a competitive tender or a cost-plus contract with an industrial partner. Incentive contracts mix the two. For instance the seller may be given a target price and the buyer and seller share any excess. However, considering the two extremes clarifies the issue. A central issue is the allocation of the risk that unpredicted problems will raise costs. The buyer takes this risk under a cost-plus contract; the seller takes this risk under a fixed-price contract. In bidding for a fixed-price contract the seller must allow for that risk by including a risk premium in the quoted price. One way the risk may be shared is if the fixed-price contract has an inflation adjustment. A contract without adjustments is known as a firm, or firm-fixed, price contract. For brevity, the term fixed-price is used for both. Indexing the contract for inflation provides insurance and, in the absence of indexation, a risk-averse contractor may include a substantial risk premium to cover the costs of unknown future inflation. In terms of administrative costs, fixed-price contracts can be difficult to write and competitions may be expensive to run while cost-plus contracts face difficulties in determining the costs incurred, the right profit rate for projects which, for the firm, are low risk and the capital employed to which the profit rate is applied.

Both fixed-price and cost-plus contracts raise what economists call principal-agent problems in the relationship between the principal (the government) and the agent (the firm providing the weapon). These problems, which are discussed below, include asymmetric information, transaction costs, moral hazard, adverse selection, risk aversion, incomplete contracts, lock-in and renegotiation.

A cost-plus contract, where the government pays the contractor's costs plus a profit margin, is flexible and can easily adjust to changing requirements. It can build up relationships and trust in the partnership, though this trust may be exploited. As Groucho Marx said, 'The secret of life is honesty and fair dealing. If you can fake that you have got it made.'

Corts and Singh (2004) use evidence from non-defence offshore drilling contracts to show that cost-plus contracts are more common if buyers and sellers have longer, more frequent interactions. Frequent interactions – what economists call a repeated game – may keep both parties honest, since they do not wish to risk losing the relationship and the benefits of future trade. Bajari, McMillan and Tadelis (2009) examine whether a buyer of a customised good should use competitive bidding or negotiation to select a contractor. On the basis of an examination of a set of private sector building contracts in Northern California, they found auctions performed poorly when projects are complex, contractual design is incomplete and there are few available bidders. They may also stifle communication between buyers and sellers. Kalnins and Mayer (2004), considering contracts from the IT services industry, find that cost-plus contracts tend to be preferred when quality is harder to observe and when costs are difficult to estimate *ex ante*.

Cost-plus provides insurance to risk-averse contractors and the defence department can reduce risk by pooling over many independent projects, but it provides no incentive to minimise costs. The partnership may create monopolies, if the incumbent acquires the specialist knowledge and IPR necessary to provide the equipment. Cost-plus can distort the make-or-buy decision, since one can apply the cost-plus profit mark-up on capital employed to what one makes but not what one buys. Formulae for the allocation of overhead costs can cause cheap items, like coffee pots, to appear incredibly expensive. In the UK there is a Single Source Regulations Office to monitor non-competitive contracts.

Having a competitive tender, with a fixed price for the specified work, is a standard economic relationship in the commercial sector and it encourages cost-minimisation by the firm if there are many potential suppliers. The defence department may not know how many potential suppliers there are and be concerned that, if there is only one bid, it may have to accept it, however high. Since not everything can be specified in advance, contracts are inevitably incomplete. While cost-plus contracts can accommodate changes easily, fixed-price cannot. They can be inflexible and expensive to renegotiate if either the defence department requirement changes or if the supplier's costs change. When the requirement changes, the defence department is in a weak bargaining position because the firm can insist on the contract. The UK coalition government that came to power in 2010 considered cancelling the two aircraft carriers under construction. But it discovered that cancellation was more expensive than continuing construction. Such contracts with high cancellation costs reassure firms that they will not be subject to the 'hold-up' or 'lock-in' problem, which is that having made the investment for the project they will be in a weak bargaining position relative to the government.

Higher costs than expected by the firm under a fixed-price contract also prompt renegotiation. In 1997 the UK MoD signed fixed-price contracts with GEC-Marconi to build a set of Astute class hunter-killer submarines in the Barrow shipyards for delivery in 2005. GEC was taken over by BAE and there were big cost overruns on the submarines. Part of the problem was that submarine building skills had been lost because of the long gap between the end of development of the previous Vanguard class and the beginning of Astute. In 2003 the contract was renegotiated. BAE had to write down its profits by £750 million because of the penalty and said that it would never accept fixed-price contracts again. Astute, the first of the class, was finally commissioned in 2010. The cost of the first three boats increased from a forecast £2.2 billion to £3.5 billion. As of late 2021, four of the seven boats have been commissioned.

Both monitoring costs for cost-plus and running competitions for fixed-price can be expensive. In competitions, the buyer has to evaluate many complex bids and the suppliers have to invest heavily in bidding. Competitions in the USA are often followed by legal challenges and prolonged litigation. Since the contracts are large relative to the firm, litigation may be a good investment for the loser. Partnerships, with bidding restricted to suppliers with established reputations, are safer and allow cost savings and quality improvements but they restrict entry, reduce competition and limit the range of solutions proposed. Collusion among the bidders in a competition is always a danger and more transparency may increase the probability of collusion, allowing price-fixing cartels to detect cheating by members more easily. Although the market may appear competitive, it may be very dependent on a single specialist subcontractor who supplies all the competing prime contractors.

Because the weapons are systems, you must have mechanisms to ensure that the contractors for the different components interact effectively, for instance that they pool patents. Separate contracts for development and production can run into IPR problems, where the firm winning the production contract is dependent on the IPR of the firm doing the development. Often the government will provide some equipment and there has to be provision in the contract for the failure of the government to provide it.

Rogerson (1995) provides a general survey of the incentive models and Rogerson (1994) discusses the use of prizes to encourage competitive innovation in the design stage. In the first stage, there is a competition to design the weapon. But the firm that wins the design stage is very likely to win the production stage because, as noted before, it will have the IPR and tacit knowledge gained during the design stage. In the production stage, the firm will then be a monopoly producer and can recoup the investment it made in the design stage. The only constraint on the incumbent is then the threat of second sourcing if it abuses its monopoly power. Second sourcing is only feasible in the USA, and perhaps Russia and China, though they also have more coercive instruments to constrain monopolists.

Contracts also have to cover the allocation of responsibility for substandard weapons. Weapons can only be rejected on the basis of technical performance standards that are specified in advance; the supplier needs to know what to provide, and that can be tested. In practice, important characteristics such as performance in combat cannot be tested, though the military hope that the technical standards will be related to combat performance. During conflict the choice is harder, since the consequence of rejecting substandard weapons is getting fewer or no weapons; in combat, even bad weapons are better than no weapons.

Cost-plus may encourage product innovation, as the firm gets paid for the R&D, whereas fixed-price may encourage process innovation, as the firm gets to keep any cost savings. A firm that cuts costs a lot on a fixed-price contract can make big profits, which may cause the defence department political problems. An old but instructive case is the guidance system on the Bloodhound missile, where there was a public outcry when it was revealed in 1964 that Ferranti made a profit of £5.7 million on a £12 million fixed-price contract and Ferranti had to repay part of this. Flower (1966) comments that an earlier Bloodhound cost-plus contract with Ferranti, where actual costs were twenty times the original estimate, aroused no public criticism or outcry and noted that fixed-price contracts should not be used on new projects or where there is a dominant supplier. Flower thought that the fact that Ferranti succeeded in producing the Bloodhound at a lower cost than the government thought possible should be a cause for congratulation, not criticism, but the firm's profit was larger than was politically acceptable on a government contract. Flower concluded that Ferranti's major mistakes were to be too efficient (if its costs had not been so low there would have been no scandal) and to believe rather naively that when the government agreed to a fixed-price contract, it would honour its terms no matter what the outcome.

5.2 Principal-Agent Issues

Although it was noted in the Introduction that the government was not a unitary actor, this section will use a standard economic model in which the government (the buyer) is the principal, and the arms firm (the seller) is the agent. This relationship involves a range of concepts regularly used by economists, given in bold.

Asymmetric information refers to the fact that the buyer and seller know different things about crucial variables, like quality or cost, which are not directly observable. Each may have incentives not to reveal what they know. There are cases where it is not in the interest of one or both of the parties to share information with each other and cases where it is in their interest but there are obstacles to communication. As a result there may be what RAND Europe (2021) refers to as misaligned assumptions, where at least one side may not be making decisions on the best available evidence about, for instance, risks. Failure to communicate information about likely risks, whether deliberate, for strategic reasons or as the inadvertent result of obstacles to communication, can lead to unrealistic expectations among the actors.

Moral hazard arises because costs and quality are determined by the effort of the seller, which the buyer cannot monitor. Cost-plus contracts provide insurance to the seller but give them less incentive to reduce costs. Fixed-price contracts provide incentives to minimise costs but the firm may do so by reducing quality, if quality is difficult to monitor. Military capability and effectiveness can be assessed, but only technical performance can be measured objectively enough to be specified in the contract. Corruption and bribery also raise issues of moral hazard. RAND Europe (2021) noted that the UK defence acquisition system is prone to moral hazard whereby poor delivery results in only limited negative consequences.

Adverse selection arises under competitive bidding because the buyer cannot discover information that is private to the selling firm and the wrong supplier may win. The same problem causes the winner's curse, in public value auctions, for the right to drill for oil, for instance. This arises because the winner, the bidder who thinks the right is more valuable than everybody else, is likely to have over-estimated its value. In competitive tenders the firm that wins may not be the lowest cost producer but the one that bid too low because they did not understand the problem and were subject to the winner's curse. Bidders should build a premium into their bids to protect them from the winner's curse. With fixed-price, if costs are higher than the winner's bid, this is just a transfer from the selling firm to the buyer. But a large transfer may not be feasible and the buyer may have to bail out the firm to get the project completed. Since the firm knows this, it has an incentive to bid low to get the buyer to commit to the project, knowing that once committed the buyer will have to complete.

The conspiracy of optimism may make the buyer happy to collude, to get the project into the plan. If the government purchase acts as a signal of the quality of the product, winning may open up other markets, for instance exports, so it may be worth bidding low. A low bid on a development contract may allow the firm to use IPR, learning curves or acquired tacit knowledge to establish monopoly power, which can be exploited to make money on production.

Transaction costs, discussed in the Introduction, play a major role in the decision as to the type of organisation to get the weapons from. Adler et al. (1998) argue that transaction costs will depend on three characteristics: asset specificity, uncertainty and how easy it is to write a contract with a private firm. The paper finds that these three characteristics predict the type of contract in a sample of US Air Force R&D contracts. The asset specificity, whether it can be used elsewhere, may refer to physical capital – for instance, can the facility only be used for supplying the defence department, as with the AWE – or human capital – transaction-specific knowledge acquired in the relationship.

Risk aversion is important, because of the size of the project and the consequences of failure. There are military, political and financial risks. The public sector may be risk-averse because of the political fall-out from failures. The firm may be risk-averse because the project is large relative to the firm. Rolls-Royce was bankrupted by the RB211 fixed-price civil engine project in 1971. Since the uncertainty surrounding military contracts is large, so is the risk premium that suppliers build into fixed-price bids; cost-plus, by providing insurance, avoids paying this risk premium.

Incomplete contracts and renegotiation are common because not every contingency can be specified in the original contract and changes in technology and buyer needs mean the contract may have to be rewritten. Crocker and Reynolds (1993) examine the efficiency of incomplete contracts for US Air Force engine procurement. There is a trade-off between the large *ex ante* costs in drafting more complete contracts and the *ex post* inefficiencies associated with less detailed specifications. Complexity and uncertainty make writing contracts hard but a record of past opportunistic behaviour or a hold-up by a sole-source contractor increases the likelihood of more complete contracts.

Credibility and reputation are important; one-off games are different from repeated games. In one-off games, there may be more incentive to behave opportunistically and take advantage of the other player than in repeated games. In repeated games, reputation is valuable because it enables the trading relationship to continue. This can solve the lock-in problem and build trust. Threats by the government may not be credible. The firm may think the government is bluffing because the firm knows that it would not be in the government's interests to carry out the threat. This means that it is important on occasion for the defence department to establish credibility by cancelling projects that are failing and penalising firms that perform poorly. Even then it may be difficult to establish credibility if the contractor knows that the project is needed by the defence department and there is no alternative supplier. Importing some systems may send credible signals to a domestic monopolist.

5.3 Concluding Comments

The optimal form of contract depends on the large number of factors discussed in this section. It is clear that there is not a single best form of contract; it will differ from case to case. In principle, the appropriate form of contract will depend on circumstances, which factors are relevant in a particular case. In practice, because of uncertainty and asymmetric information, the defence department does not know which factors are relevant. This point, that there is no single solution, is made by Hambleton et al. (2013), authors of DEG (2005), who warn that the MoD must 'beware of a blanket adoption of popular nostrums such as competition, privatisation, taut budget management, etc., which might work well in some, but not all, parts of MOD'.

The fact that different types of firm may prefer a cost-plus contract for different reasons provides an illustration of the uncertainties. The firm may be very efficient but highly risk-averse, perhaps because it is small and fears that it may be bankrupted by a fixed-price contract if some technical problem proves very expensive to solve. The cost-plus contract gives it confidence to bid. Alternatively, the firm may be very inefficient and prefer the cost-plus contract because it will not be penalised for its lack of effort. While a cost-plus contract should go to the first but not the second type, the MoD cannot objectively determine which type the firm is, though it may learn through repeated interaction.

The belief that there is a single best form of contract can lead to a long cycle between forms which runs over decades. As the defence department slowly gains experience with one form of contract, say cost-plus, they increasingly discover its limitations. Learning is slow because of the length of time required by the procurement process, which means that it takes many years to discover the problems with the contract. After these problems are revealed, the alternative form of contract, competitive tendering, starts to look increasingly attractive. They start to switch to the alternative and, as the competitive procurement contracts mature, they discover the problems with competition. The cycle then starts again.

6 Buyer Organisation: What Are the Problems?

The efficiency of the procurement system will depend on the effectiveness of the buyer, the government. The previous section took a standard model in which the government, the buyer, is the principal and the seller, the arms firm, is the agent. But this simplifies the complex nature of the process because, as noted in the Introduction, the government is not a unitary decision-maker. Among economists, two visions of the state exist in uneasy conjunction. One is of the state as a rational actor that can make decisions about issues such as the maintenance of a defence industrial and technology base. The other is of the state as an arena for conflict among a set of warring tribes subject to institutional constraints such as constitutional rules and standard operating procedures. The tribes include the politicians, elected or otherwise, the military and the bureaucracy, each of which will have warring tribes within it.

Hierarchy creates horizontal barriers between different levels of the bureaucracy. There may be incentives to tell superiors what they want to hear rather than what they need to know. There are also vertical barriers, often labelled silos. These are separate sections with their own interests that are reluctant to share information and do not communicate effectively. The failure of the FBI and CIA to communicate effectively contributed to the failure to stop the 9/11 attacks. In defence departments there are very strong vertical barriers, not just between the military and the civilians but within each group. This section begins with the relationship between the military and civilians in the procurement process and then goes on to more general people issues within the procurement process.

6.1 Who Is in Control? France and the UK

Section 2 raised the question of whether requirements were best set by the military or by the procurement professionals, typically engineers. In the USA and the UK the military play a significant role in the procurement process while in France procurement professionals play a relatively more important role. The British procurement body, Defence Equipment and Support (DE&S), is much less powerful than its French equivalent, the DGA. As noted above, the DGA acts as a patron for the industry, using procurement and export promotion as part of a coherent industrial strategy developed over decades, in which defence firms, mainly state-owned, have considerable freedom to develop weapons they think will sell abroad. To a certain extent the armed forces and politicians were marginalised by technocratic professional engineers trained at the Ecole Polytechnique who moved between the arms firms and the DGA. French citizens at the Polytechnique would also normally serve in the military. The classic source on the French system is Kolodziej (1987). Kapstein and Oudot (2009, p. 10) comment that 'Although the book was published twenty years ago its analysis of the DGA and the French procurement system remains compelling.'

There is the obvious benefit in giving the military a significant role since they will use the weapons. But there are costs. For military officers, the posting to procurement is usually for two years, a small part of their career and not an important part for promotion prospects. In the UK and USA the emphasis is on meeting the career concerns of the military and giving them experience of the procurement process, not optimising the procurement process itself. This is not necessarily wrong, but there are trade-offs. The officer begins the two-year posting with very little background or training in the details of procurement or often of the particular weapons system, which may be used by a different part of their service: an infantry officer may know little about artillery. The officers spend the best part of the first year learning about the project and procedures, may make a few changes to show that they have had an impact and will spend much of their second year preoccupied with their next posting.

The National Audit Office (NAO 2021) noted that the median running time for the projects and programmes it considered was 77 months, while the median time in post for the senior responsible owner (SRO) of the project, was 22 months. The SRO, who is usually a military figure, is responsible for ensuring that the project or programme meets its objectives and realises the expected benefits.

In terms of the efficiency of the weapons procurement system, Kapstein and Oudot (2009) argue that France, where the procurement professionals play a more significant role, seems to have managed procurement better than Britain. They say:

> Beginning in the early 1990s, France embarked on a series of policy reforms that enabled the state to contain skyrocketing weapons costs. We emphasise three, inter-related aspects of the defence acquisition environment in France that favoured cost containment: first, hard budget constraints; second the great technical capacity that the French government brought to bear on the weapons acquisition process, coupled with its iterative relationship with a small number of suppliers; and third the use of contracting techniques that empowered project managers.

Because of the more positive attitude to the state, and to engineers, in France than the UK, the human capital available to the French state was greater than in the UK, where the best and the brightest tended to gravitate to finance rather than government. Nevertheless, there have been major problems with the development of some French weapons systems, including the Charles de Gaulle nuclear-powered aircraft carrier.

In the UK, Bernard Gray, who wrote a scathing report on British procurement and subsequently became Chief of Defence Materiel, said in evidence to the House of Commons Defence Committee in January 2010 that when he began the review he was told by the Treasury (the UK finance ministry) that there were three main problems. Firstly the defence programme was substantially out of balance. Secondly there was a lack of clarity and leadership in the MoD head office, particularly at the top of the organisation, and a lack of accountability and responsibility. Thirdly there were insufficient skills inside the procurement organisation, DE&S, to discharge the job. Lord Levene, in his independent report to the MoD on Defence Reform, identified a structural 'inability to take tough, timely decisions in the Defence interest, particularly those necessary to ensure financial control and an affordable defence programme' (Levene 2011, p. 13). There is some debate about whether responsibility for this recurrent imbalance between aspirations and resources should be attributed to planning failures by the MoD or to political failures by successive governments who were unwilling to make hard choices.

Lord Currie, in his independent report to the MoD on non-competitive pricing in the UK, made very similar points to Kapstein and Oudot (2009) about the technical experience of the French DGA staff relative to their British equivalents (Currie 2011, pp. 52 & 139). But Currie rejected a move towards the French system of a more legally formalised contracting system and fewer changes in requirements, because of the strong differences in culture and preferences between the two systems. Hard budget constraints, cancelling projects that went over time or budget, would provide the right incentives against the optimism bias but may not be credible in the UK. Currie notes that in the USA programmes should be cancelled if a 25 per cent overrun occurs, but they rarely are cancelled since the Secretary of Defense can override this by submitting a report detailing why the programme is essential.

Another possible reason for limiting the role of the military in procurement is inter-service rivalry. The promotion prospects of the officer in the procurement posting will depend not on the military as a whole but on the particular armed service that the officer belongs to. The armed forces interpret policy in the light of the organisational culture and operational roles of their particular service: army, navy, air force or, in the USA, marines. Inter-service rivalry then becomes a major factor in budgeting and procurement. The services will fight over the allocation of limited funds, and choices over roles, missions and weapons systems. When nuclear weapons became available, in the countries that had them, all three services tried to get them. Weapons systems that are used by all three services, like helicopters, are used in quite different ways. There can be conflicts where one service is supposed to support another but the two have different views of their appropriate role. The US Army likes the A10 'Warthog', a slow, heavily armoured close air support aircraft which is very effective and popular with ground troops. The US Air Force does not like the A10 because it is slow and ugly, and has repeatedly tried to find excuses to take it out of service, only to be overruled by Congress. Donnithorne (2017) discusses how civil–military relations interact with single service cultures.

6.2 People

One of the heuristics in DEG (2005, p. 264), which is from an engineer's perspective, is 'Systems don't go wrong. It's the people involved that do. Improve the quality of the people and you will improve the systems they build.'

Issues of tenure, military and civilians only staying in the job for a short period, training and recruitment come up repeatedly in criticisms of the procurement process. Whereas the government procurement officers in the USA and UK are probably there for a two-year posting, their industry counterparts are likely to be working on the project for its whole lifetime, which averages about seven years but is often much longer. In addition, people with skills in negotiation and financial management are highly prized in industry and the government often cannot pay enough to recruit or retain people with those skills. In the UK there have been regular complaints about the lack of qualified accountants at the MoD. Having procurement officers staying in the same post for the duration of the project may build up trust and understanding between the procurement officer and industry but may foster corrupt relationships if the procurement officer expects to get a subsequent job in industry.

Procurement officers need to have enough time to do a good job. Warren (2014) points out that composing a carefully constructed and detailed contract takes time, in both planning and execution. Contracting officers who have a limited time budget must divide their time among the contracting tasks at hand. If the number of tasks increases, less time will necessarily be devoted to each, often leaving some contingencies unaddressed. The choice to leave contracts less complete may also affect the pricing structure, the extent of competition and the final price paid. Warren estimates the effect of workload spikes caused by the retirement of other procurement officers on the selection of procurement terms. In a sample of 150,000 contracts from eight-five procurement offices over eleven years, increases in workload reduce the use of competitive acquisition procedures and firm-fixed-price contracts, increase the risk of renegotiation and increase costs. Busier contracting officers choose to write less complete contracts, leading to more renegotiations as unspecified eventualities arrive. Anticipating these costly renegotiations, the officers decrease their use of fixed-price contracts, which are more difficult to renegotiate than cost-plus contracts.

Morale and motivation may matter. Spenkuch et al. (2021) examine the effect of ideological misalignment between US procurement officers and the president. They use a very detailed dataset, which includes political affiliation, individual contracts, which are not just for defence, and the procurement officer responsible. Misalignment, for instance a Democratic procurement officer under a Republican president, increases cost overruns by about 8 per cent on average, after controlling for other factors. They interpret this as a morale effect whereby bureaucrats are more motivated and exert more effort when they are more aligned with the organisational mission. They use cost overruns as a measure of performance.

At an individual level, it is difficult to know whether a particular cost overrun is due to lack of effort on the part of a procurement officer or other factors. Output is difficult to measure, each project is unique and it is difficult to determine who was responsible for failure, given the complex subcontracting and supply chains. Trying to determine who was responsible may also delay the project. As a result, high-powered incentives, like sacking people, may not work and may be counterproductive, not allowing learning from experience, particularly bad experiences. Learning from failures can be useful (Yu 2021). A strong culture of blame and punishment also provides incentives to hide problems, which again inhibits learning from experience. Lack of institutional memory is a constant complaint in investigations, which repeatedly report that there is little learning from experience gained on previous projects, so mistakes get repeated. There is some evidence of learning from experience on the project itself but, as Bismarck is supposed to have said, 'Only a fool learns from his own mistakes. The wise man learns from the mistakes of others.'

There is a range of other tensions. Is it better to provide strict rules or give considerable discretion to empower project managers? Discretion allows adaptability at the cost of control. Rules make co-ordination between departments or systems easier. But in this whole process, the people are central.

6.3 Concluding Comments

Organisational culture matters. Reforms that do not fit with the culture do not embed. The differences between the French and UK cultures with respect to defence include different attitudes to the state and different attitudes to engineers.

There is no equivalent to the Ecole Polytechnique in the UK – the Defence Academy is a quite different sort of institution. Thus, even if the French procurement system were thought more effective than the British system, it could not be imported into the UK because the culture and institutions are different.

7 Externalities: Are There Spill-Overs?

There is a general question as to whether defence policy, and procurement in particular, should be driven purely by defence objectives or whether it should take account of wider economic consequences of the spending. These include the spill-over effects on factors like employment, technology and regional development. These spill-overs are what economists call externalities: indirect consequences of the defence spending. Since defence budgets are large, these spill-overs are large. This general question of the interaction between the military and the wider economy will be addressed first with a UK example.

7.1 Prosperity

The 2015 Strategic Defence and Security Review set out the UK's three National Security Objectives (NSO). These were NSO1: Protect Our People, NSO2: Project Our Global Influence and NSO3: Promote Our Prosperity. Protection and power projection are traditional tasks for defence departments but promoting prosperity has usually been left to the finance ministry or industry ministry, which have more economic expertise and policy instruments specifically designed to attain economic objectives like prosperity. While the defence budget and defence procurement have economic effects, it is not clear that they are effective economic instruments to promote prosperity.

Thus the 2015 elevation of promoting prosperity to NSO3 provoked some concern. There were two particular concerns. The first concern was with goal displacement, the danger that trying to meet economic objectives would distract the MoD from the already difficult calculations it faced in meeting military objectives. Economists argue that one needs the same number of instruments as objectives in order to achieve each objective. When there are fewer instruments than objectives, in principle there can be trade-offs between objectives. For example, a central bank can set the monetary policy instrument, such as the interest rate, to achieve a little less unemployment at the cost of a little more inflation. Such trade-offs are controversial among economists and as a result some central banks, like the Bank of England, are given a single mandate, to control inflation. The US Federal Reserve has what is called a dual mandate from Congress to 'promote effectively the goals of maximum employment, stable prices, and moderate long term interest rates'.

Just as the Federal Reserve is given a dual mandate, one might give the defence department a dual mandate to consider the benefit of a little more employment at the cost of a little less military effectiveness. But this assumes that the defence department can fine-tune the trade-off between the objectives: a little bit more of one, a little bit less of the other. Instead it may be a matter of either hitting or missing the objective, in which case trying to achieve multiple objectives is like trying to hit two targets with a single missile. This can be a recipe for disaster and it may be better to do one thing (buy weapons) properly than two things (buy weapons and promote employment) badly.

A second concern was the danger that, in weapons procurement, the MoD's bargaining position with a domestic monopolist would be weakened. If the firm could argue that prosperity promotion required the MoD to buy British, the competitive constraint and leverage provided by the MoD's ability to import would be reduced.

Economists have long taken it for granted that defence does promote prosperity to the extent that it contributes to providing security, safety from threats. In 1776, in *The Wealth of Nations*, Adam Smith argued that it was the duty of the sovereign to protect the nation from external violence, to protect its members from injustice and oppression of each other and to maintain public works and institutions. Economists since then have argued that if people do not believe that their life, liberty and property are safe, they will not have the confidence or incentives to consume, invest and trade, with the consequence that economic activity will collapse.

Defence makes a direct contribution to prosperity to the extent that it protects the nation from external violence and provides the internal security that is necessary for the economy to flourish. Security is a necessary but not a sufficient condition for the economy to flourish; other things are also required and most economic theory is about these other things. The lack of any UK productivity growth in the decade after 2010 is probably not a result of lack of security. While insecure economies do not prosper and there is a large literature on the economic costs of conflict, measuring the value of peacetime defence is a more difficult question than measuring the cost of conflict. Both require comparing an observed case with a hypothetical counterfactual. The counterfactual to an observed conflict is peace and it is less difficult to calculate what peace might have been like during a conflict than to calculate what conflict might have been like during peace. Whereas there is only one sort of peace, there are many types of potential conflict that might be considered as counterfactuals.

This direct contribution of defence to prosperity, through providing security, is distinct from any indirect contribution to prosperity that defence might make were it, for instance, to generate employment or arms exports, reduce regional disparities, improve productivity through technological spin-off or increase human capital from military training that provides skills valued in the wider economy. The distinction between direct and indirect rests on the fact that promoting security is a direct objective driving defence policy. Boosting employment and exports or promoting technology are not direct objectives but positive externalities from the defence budget – indirect benefits of the primary objective, to defend the country. There are also negative externalities – indirect costs, like pollution and nuclear contamination, environmental degradation and heavy use of fossil fuels.

7.2 Employment

Defence departments generate a lot of employment both through the military and civil servants on their payroll and through their expenditure. Procurement, expenditure on equipment, will have a direct effect on the employment of the prime contractor and subcontractors and an indirect effect as those employees spend their earnings, generating other jobs. These employment effects will differ depending on the capital intensity of the equipment produced and whether it is a domestic or imported product. Estimates of these employment effects are often quoted but they are difficult to estimate and very uncertain, so have large confidence intervals. Certain areas around military bases or defence factories, where there is little alternative work, can be very dependent on jobs generated by military spending. Procurement decisions can be swayed by employment consequences, particularly if they impact on politically important localities and when the politicians involved are more sensitive to the short-term political advantages than the long-term military consequences.

Arms firms are aware of this and often emphasise how many jobs will be created by the project. In the United States, where Congress has a considerable influence on procurement, firms can often identify the jobs generated in each electoral district. The employment effects of military spending are very context-dependent. If there is full employment, more workers on military projects mean fewer workers on other projects. After World War I in the UK the reduction in military spending was associated with mass unemployment. But this was primarily a consequence of the deflationary economic policy of trying to return to the gold standard at the pre-war exchange rate. Government spending got Germany out of the inter-war depression but this was initially for the construction of the autobahn system rather than the subsequent re-armament. However, in the UK and USA increased military spending did end the high inter-war unemployment. After World War II, contrary to expectations, full employment was maintained. This was despite military spending in the USA and UK falling from a wartime peak of over 50 per cent of GDP to below 10 per cent.

There has been an argument, particularly on the Left, that military expenditures have been adjusted to maintain full employment in western countries. This is known as the military Keynesianism hypothesis. As has been noted, military expenditure can create employment but there are many more effective ways of creating employment than spending on the military. As with the autobahn, infrastructure spending can create more jobs than military spending, but even targeting infrastructure spending effectively is difficult. The reductions of military expenditure in the USA and UK after the end of the Cold War saw full employment, budget surpluses and the macro-economic stability labelled the Great Moderation. Overall, it is not clear that military spending is necessary, effective or in fact utilised for employment creation.

There are substantial empirical problems in estimating the effect of military spending, or government spending in general, on national income, output or employment. The difficulty is that the linkages go both ways: as income increases, more is spent on the military. Estimates of the fiscal multiplier, the value of the change in output that results from a dollar change in government expenditure, vary from large positive effects to large negative effects. The large positive effects in the USA tend to depend on the effects of the Korean and Vietnam wars. Dunne and Smith (1990), looking at a panel of OECD countries, find no relationship between the share of military spending and the unemployment rate.

An alternative approach is to use local data where two-way causation is less important. Auerbach et al. (2019) link detailed US city-level data on purchases by the DOD, wages, hours, employment, establishments and GDP to study the effects of a fiscal stimulus. They find that GDP increases by more than the increase in DOD spending and try to relate the other responses to standard economic theories. The labour share of income is relatively constant; measured labour productivity increases; the increase in hours worked is primarily due to higher employment; the real product wage increases and the real worker wage falls owing to a sharp increase in local rental prices. Accompanying the fall in real worker wages is an increase in local consumption that, along with the increase in hours, contributes to a sharp decline in the household labour wedge. (The labour wedge is the ratio of the marginal rate of substitution of consumption for leisure to the marginal product of labour.) The paper tries to provide an explanation for this combination of responses, which are not what standard theory would suggest.

7.3 Technology

The output a society can produce depends on its land, representing crucial though often unpriced environmental services, its capital, its labour and the technology available, which will depend on the scientific and engineering skills available to the society. Since there are strong links between the military and society, there will be links between the military and civilian science and engineering, and the links go both ways.

The Global Positioning System (GPS) is a military system that has very wide civil applications. It was also a technology that was crucial to the military in the 1991 Gulf War. When GPS was initially proposed, one reaction is said to have been: 'I know where I am, why do I need a satellite to tell me where I am?' But armies are notorious for getting lost; there is an old army observation, 'the most dangerous thing in the world is an officer with a map'. But GPS changed that and proved its military worth in the 1991 Gulf War. A British general, asked about the effect of GPS, responded: 'It was the first time in my life that when a subaltern told me where he was, I could believe him.' Armies have always had difficulty navigating in deserts and the war could not have been fought in the way it was without GPS.

Originally GPS had been a purely military system but from 1983 President Reagan allowed civilian use, which grew rapidly and a commercial market in receivers developed. Before the Gulf War most military vehicles did not have GPS but it could be rapidly fitted using commercial receivers. Most of these were made in Japan but the Buy America Act prevented US forces from buying them. However, the Japanese government bought a large number and gave them to the USA as its contribution to the war. Most of the friendly fire incidents in the Gulf War, where allied forces attacked each other by mistake, involved vehicles without GPS.

The gap between the science, technology and engineering used by the military and by the rest of society plays a central role in the spill-overs. During World War II the gap was quite small: civilian factories could be switched to producing tanks and aircraft. After the war the gap widened: military equipment became increasingly specialised and different. Then the gap narrowed again as civilian technology overtook military technology and the military started to buy COTS equipment. Even arcane technologies that had once been the sole preserve of the military and the intelligence community, such as cryptography, became dominated by civilian research because of their commercial importance, particularly in finance.

Whereas once there was spin-off from military to civilian technology, increasingly the military gets the technology from commercial sources – spin-in rather than spin-off. Rather than having the defence industry design and build special-ised electronic components and software for them, the military now rely on standard components from commercial suppliers. The Department of Defense (DOD 2022) notes that this raises security concerns since these commercial suppliers are foreign, often Chinese. There is also a problem with timescales. The life cycle of commercial electronics is about two years, driven by Moore's Law that the number of transistors on an integrated circuit doubles roughly every two years. The average military procurement time is about seven years, almost four generations of electronics. This means that when the military system goes into service, the electronics are not merely obsolete but often no longer even in production. Since military systems may be in service for thirty years or more, obtaining spares and replacements can be difficult. The US DOD established a facility to produce obsolete electronic chips no longer in commercial production but still in military use. The gaps between military and commercial technology and timescales have implications for rapid mobilisation and the provision of urgent operational requirements.

The extent of the spin-off of technology from the military to the rest of society is controversial with strong positions on both sides. Vernon W. Ruttan (2006), an expert on innovation, asks *Is War Necessary for Economic Growth?* He concludes that the answer is yes, though his argument has been widely criticised. With the end of the Cold War, the 1990s was a decade of cutting military spending and a period of rapid technological innovation. While many technologies have military or wartime origins, many have not. If a large part of national resources and R&D is devoted to the military, as it was during the World Wars and Cold War, it is not surprising that many technologies have military origins. Currently, defence R&D is the largest component of publicly funded R&D in the USA, UK and France. However, had those resources been spent on civil R&D, without the secrecy restrictions and diversion of scarce scientific and technical skills to the military, there may have been even more innovations. The counter-argument is that, in the absence of the military pressure, those resources would not have been spent on R&D. In both military and civil research, how the government invests is crucial and Mazzucato (2013) discusses the effectiveness of government innovation.

Moretti et al. (2021) examine the impact of government funding for R&D – and defence-related R&D in particular – on privately conducted R&D, and its ultimate effect on productivity growth. They relate privately funded R&D to lagged government-funded R&D using industry-country-level data from OECD countries and firm-level data from France. In both datasets, they find evidence of 'crowding in' rather than 'crowding out', as increases in government-funded R&D for an industry or a firm result in significant increases in private sector

R&D in that industry or firm. They also find evidence of international spill-overs, as increases in government-funded R&D in a particular industry and country raise private R&D in the same industry in other countries. Finally, they find that increases in private R&D induced by increases in defence R&D result in productivity gains. To deal with possible reverse causality they use defence R&D, which they regard as exogenous, as an instrument. They note that the effect is not large and does not necessarily imply that defence R&D is the most efficient way for a government to stimulate private sector innovation and productivity.

The military origins of many technologies are not necessarily an argument for support of military R&D. The fact that DARPA produced the Internet is given as an argument for supporting military research but the fact that CERN, the European organisation for nuclear research in Geneva, produced the World Wide Web is rarely given as a reason to support research into particle physics. If you want to promote technology there are generally better and less expensive ways to do it than relying on the military to spin it off. In any event, it is quite difficult for governments to target innovation effectively. Consider the growth of India as a major software producer. Partly this was the result of an education system that produced very good software engineers, many of whom now run US high technology firms. But partly this was because the Indian government did not treat software as a serious industry. Software benefited from not having the extensive government support and intervention that doomed many other Indian industries, particularly in manufacturing, including the defence industry. Despite heavy investments, the development of Indian combat aircraft has been very slow. The capacity of the state, the quality of its decisions and bureaucracy, is central to effective intervention.

7.4 Civil–Military Interactions

Many military activities became central to wider society: mapping (the name of the UK organisation Ordnance Survey reflects its military origin), meteorology, air traffic control, the Internet and GPS. Often, as their civilian importance grows, they are spun off from the military, like mapping and meteorology in the UK. There is a large scientific and engineering component to a range of things that the military do for the wider society: search and rescue, coastguards, protection of oil rigs and aid to the civil power in times of emergency. This aid can include maintaining bio-security during pandemics, providing support during natural disasters like floods, maintaining public order during large scale disruptions or, in a previous generation, planning to run the country after a nuclear war. To fulfil these functions the military need the skills to interact with the wider society and to have a broad spectrum of technological capabilities. It may be useful to have the military provide these functions but societies without armed forces, like Iceland and Costa Rica, provide these services in other ways than the military.

The military often leave the armed forces at a comparatively young age and have careers later in civil society, taking their skills with them. In Israel, people who worked in Unit 8200, the military signals intelligence organisation, went on to establish a range of technology firms. There are examples like management education and logistics where commercial firms have learned from the military. General William Gus Pagonis went from organising the logistics of the 1991 Gulf War to using his skills in the private sector. Doctors trained by the military take their skills back to civilian life and military medicine has been the source of many innovations, particularly in the treatment of traumatic injuries and prosthetics.

There is a debate about the merits of the 'revolving door' which takes military and defence department civil servants into industry, particularly the defence industry, and sometimes back again into government. Lord Levene has moved back and forth a number of times. Recruited by Margaret Thatcher from a defence company to run procurement, he went back into the private sector and then returned to produce a report on the structure and management of the MoD (Levene 2011). On the one hand, the revolving door improves communications and makes efficient use of skills acquired on both sides of the door. On the other hand, there is the danger that expectations of employment in the private sector after retirement may influence decisions made while serving in government or the military and the danger that after leaving they use confidential information and personal contacts which they acquired while serving to promote the interests of the firm that hired them. It is an important issue. In many countries, senior military and defence civil servants join arms companies after retirement and there are procedures to try and minimise any negative effects of the revolving door.

In the UK, when former ministers or senior crown appointments take up a new appointment within two years of leaving service they must apply to the Office of the Advisory Committee on Business Appointments. As an example, it considered an application in 2015 from Sir Peter Wall, a former Chief of the General Staff, head of the army, who had an engineering background, to become a non-executive director at General Dynamics. The firm had contracts worth about £5.8 billion with the MoD, including the Ajax armoured vehicle discussed in Section 1, and he had official dealings with the firm during his last two years of service. The Committee allowed the appointment subject to a number of conditions which restricted what he could do during the two years after leaving the army. These included not using privileged information from his time in government, not lobbying the government, not providing advice on the terms of bids or contracts relating to the MoD and not having any involvement with matters relating to the Ajax contract.

One of the civil–military interactions of concern is an alliance of the armed services, the arms industries and members of the legislature to promote defence spending. This alliance was labelled the military-industrial complex by Dwight D. Eisenhower, the Republican US President (1953–61) and Supreme Commander of Allied Forces in Europe during World War II. In his farewell speech to the nation in 1961 he warned the USA to guard against the acquisition of influence, whether sought or unsought, by the military-industrial complex. Although it has since gained left-wing associations, he had a very conservative concern. This was the danger that coalitions of vested interests could exploit the special nature of decision-making about military matters to shape choices against peaceful goals and national security interests. They would do this in order to extract funds for their own purposes – what economists call unproductive rent-seeking. These coalitions could include members of the armed services, of the civilian defence bureaucracy, of the legislature, of the arms manufacturers and their workers. These are the transmission mechanism by which perceptions of the threat and the economic opportunity costs are translated into particular budgets or systems. These operate not just nationally but internationally and their power varies. Dunne (1995) discusses the relationship between the military-industrial complex and the defence industrial base.

7.5 Concluding Comments

Because the military is intertwined in society, absorbing substantial resources, it does have effects on employment and technology but there are more effective ways of influencing them than by military spending. There are strong scientific and engineering links between military and society but they are complicated, operate in both directions and are difficult to manage. Acquiring the technology the military need and acquiring weapons are difficult enough when the objective is buying the best value military capability. The GAO and NAO regularly document the problems in doing this. If the procurement process is further complicated by trying to fine-tune the economic spin-offs to employment, technology or regional development, there is a danger that the decision-makers will be incapacitated by the complexity of their objectives, resulting in even worse procurement decisions.

8 Conclusion

Given the uncertainties, moral hazards and large expenditures involved, it is tempting to construct elaborate 'rational' decision-making procedures. These tend to emphasise process rather than outcomes and it is not clear that they produce better decisions. Excessive regulations can cause more problems than they solve and those involved in procurement regularly complain that they are 'drowning in process', as Kincaid (2008) reports. The best projects seem marked by unified authority, sharp trade-offs and flexibility – characteristics that formal processes do not provide. Projects are easier if there is a single objective. This may be a performance goal, as with the Manhattan project to build the atomic bomb; a time goal, as with UORs; or a cost goal, where price is treated as an independent variable and specified in advance. The problem with most projects is that they have multiple goals, which have to be traded off.

Fox (2011, pp. 191–2) concludes that, while the attempted procurement reforms promoted sound management practices, these practices were not widely adopted because they were inconsistent with the very basic and strongly reinforced incentives to continue the production and development of a weapon system. For instance, the resistance to fly-before-buy and testing was a logical reaction to the additional time and up-front cost required and to the reality that testing could jeopardise acquisition programmes. Fox also notes that the short tenures of high-level DOD acquisition executives make it difficult for them to change the incentives because other participants can wait out the reforms they oppose. Procurement managers need technical and commercial skills that they rarely have, to negotiate both with contractors and with other parts of government. Some features that Fox emphasises are US-specific, including the role of Congress. Other countries where the legislature has less influence also have problems with procurement, so it cannot all be blamed on Congress.

Hambleton et al. (2013), authors of DEG (2005), argue for the need for senior officials to ensure that all their staff across the many disparate disciplines and specialist subjects are sufficiently convinced to pull in the same direction, rather than to indulge in the traditional tribal warfare and point-scoring. This will require investment in education, training and experience for acquisition staff, who must be given the necessary knowledge and ability to interact with all other relevant disciplines while still retaining the depth of expertise in their own specialisms. They must also be allowed longer periods in post in order to provide better project continuity and to enable them to practise their skills effectively.

The proposed reforms suggest that defence departments need to:

- Hire good people, train them and give them the time, resources and freedom to do a good job.
- Keep the project management and cost assurance people in post for longer to enhance their skills and provide suitable rewards to prevent them being poached or bribed by the contractors.

- Invest in technology demonstrators to show that the systems work before committing to the project and signing the production contract: fly before you buy.
- Have a rigorous, independent, 'red-team' scrutiny of projected cost, time and performance targets.
- Go back to similar projects in the past and learn from experience. Try to embed the learning and change the incentives to avoid transitory initiatives that are subsequently forgotten.
- Focus on identifying and managing risks from the start and build in a large contingency reserve.
- Try to avoid simultaneous development and production.
- Constantly monitor performance in terms of value for money and military effectiveness.
- Provide a credible threat of cancellation if the project does not meet projected time, cost and performance targets. This will provide an incentive against over-optimistic projections and offset the conspiracy of optimism between buyers and sellers. To make this credible requires cancelling projects more often.
- Penalise contractors that have performed poorly in the past by excluding them from contracts.
- Provide a credible threat to domestic monopolists by importing.
- Try to avoid changing specifications during the development and production process.
- Try to avoid varying production schedules and quantities procured to fit into fluctuating budgets for short-term affordability reasons.

All of these suggested reforms run into immediate obstacles. There is always the argument that 'This time is different'. The systems are needed quickly so there is no time for technology demonstrators. Cancelling the system means that a capability is missing. Importing means that one may lose the domestic development and production capability. The threat changes so the specifications have to change. There are political and personnel problems with the suggested staff reforms. While in some cases these objections are valid, in other cases they are smokescreens for bureaucratic inertia and vested interests. But the combination of the difficulty of the problem and the organisational dynamics that resist change has meant that the various attempts at reform have not led to much improvement.

Buying major weapons systems is inherently difficult because of uncertainties about the evolution of the threat and of the technology. It is made more difficult by the structure of the market and the incentives generated by the complicated relationship between the single buyer, the government, and the arms firms, often a domestic monopolist. There are incentives for the military and industry to be over-optimistic about time, costs and performance. There are incentives for lobbying and bribery to distort decisions towards individual rather than national interests. Given all these difficulties, one might think that the military are lucky to have any working weapons at all.

References

Adler, Terry R., Robert F. Scherer, Sydney L. Barton and Ralph Katerberg (1998) An empirical test of transaction cost theory: validating contract typology, *Journal of Applied Management Studies*, 7(2), 185–200.

Akam, Simon (2021) *The Changing of the Guard*, paperback edition, London: Scribe Publications.

Ansari, Irfan (2019) Efficient and effective management of defence resources, chapter 3 of Matthews (2019a), 47–70.

Arreguin-Toft, Ivan (2005) *How the Weak Win Wars, a Theory of Asymmetric Conflict*, Cambridge Studies in International Relations, Cambridge, UK: Cambridge University Press.

Auerbach, Alan J., Yuriy Gorodnichenko and Daniel Murphy (2019) Macroeconomic frameworks, NBER Working Paper 26365.

Augustine, Norman (1987) *Augustine's Laws*, New York: Penguin.

Bajari, Patrick, Robert McMillan and Steven Tadelis (2009) Auctions versus negotiations in procurement: an empirical analysis, *The Journal of Law, Economics, and Organization*, 25(2), 372–99.

Bongers, Aneli and Jose L. Torres (2014) Technological change in US jet fighter aircraft, *Research Policy*, 43, 1570–81.

Braddon, Derek (2019) Economic and political dimensions of the defence industry supply chain revolution, chapter 14 of Matthews (2019a), 307–31.

Carril, Rodrigo and Mark Duggan (2020) The impact of industry consolidation on government procurement: evidence from Department of Defense contracting, *The Journal of Public Economics*, 184, 1–17.

Castle, Jennifer L., Michael P. Clements and David F. Hendry (2019) *Forecasting: An Essential Introduction*, New Haven, CT and London: Yale University Press.

Chalmers, Malcolm, Neil Davies, Keith Hartley and C. Wilkinson (2002) The economic costs and benefits of UK defence exports, *Fiscal Studies*, 23, 343–67.

Chin, Warren (2004) *British Weapons Acquisitions Policy and the Futility of Reform*, Aldershot, UK: Ashgate.

Corts, Kenneth S. and Jasjit Singh (2004) The effect of repeated interaction on contract choice: evidence from offshore drilling, *The Journal of Law, Economics, and Organization*, 20(1), 230–60.

Coulomb, Fanny and Jacques Fontanel (2005) An economic interpretation of French military expenditures, *Defence and Peace Economics*, 16(4), 297–315.

Crocker, Keith J. and Kenneth J. Reynolds (1993) The efficiency of incomplete contracts: an empirical analysis of air force engine procurement, *RAND Journal of Economics*, 24(1), 126–46.

CRS (2022) F-35 Joint Strike Fighter (JSF) Program Updated January 14, 2022, Congressional Research Service, RL30563.

Currie, David (2011) *Review of Single Source Pricing Regulations*, London: The Stationery Office.

Dal Bó, Ernesto (2006) Regulatory capture: a review, *Oxford Review of Economic Policy*, 22(2), 203–25.

DEG (2005) *Conquering Complexity: Lessons for Defence Systems Acquisition*, The Defence Engineering Group, London: The Stationery Office.

DOD (2022) *State of Competition within the Defense Industrial Base*, Department of Defense Report, Washington DC: Office of the Under Secretary of Defense for Acquisition and Sustainment.

Donnithorne, Jeffrey W. (2017) Principled agents: the role of service culture in civil-military relations, *Orbis*, 61(4), 506–26.

Dunne, J.Paul (1995) The defense industrial base, chapter 14 of Hartley and Sandler (1995), 399–430.

Dunne, J.Paul, Maria Garcia-Alonso, Paul Levine and Ron P. Smith (2007) Determining the defence industrial base, *Defence and Peace Economics*, 18 (3), 199–221.

Dunne, J.Paul and Elizabeth Skons (2021) New technology and the US MIC, *Economics of Peace and Security Journal*, 16(2), 5–17.

Dunne, J.Paul and Ron P. Smith (1990) Military expenditure and unemployment in the OECD, *Defence Economics*, 1(1), 57–74.

Feinstein, Andrew (2011) *The Shadow World: Inside the Global Arms Trade*, London: Penguin.

Flower, J. F. (1966) The case of the profitable Bloodhound, *Accounting Research*, 4(1), 16–36.

Flyvbjerg, Bent (2014) What you should know about megaprojects and why: an overview, *Project Management Journal*, 45(2), 6–19.

Fox, J. Ronald (2011) *Defense Acquisition Reform, 1960–2009: An Elusive Goal*, Washington DC: Center of Military History, US Army.

GAO (2021) F-35, Cost and schedule risks in modernization program echo long-standing challenges, Statement of Jon Ludwigson, GAO-21-105282.

Giry, Benoit and Andy Smith (2020) Defence capability in the UK since 2010: explaining change in procurement practices, *British Politics*, 15, 433–55.

Hambleton, Ken, Ian Holder and David Kirkpatrick (2013) *Defence Acquisition – Ten Challenges*, London: mimeo.

Hartley, Keith (2017) *The Economics of Arms*, Newcastle: Agenda Publishing.

Hartley, Keith (2019) The political economy of arms collaboration, chapter 11 of Matthews (2019a), 235–57.

Hartley, Keith and Todd Sandler, editors (1995) *Handbook of Defense Economics, Volume 1*, Amsterdam: Elsevier.

HCDC (2021) *Obsolescent and Outgunned: The British Army's Armoured Vehicle Capability*, House of Commons Defence Committee, House of Commons, March.

HCL (2020) *A Brief Guide to Previous British Defence Reviews*, House of Commons Library, Briefing paper 07313, 26 February.

Hennessy, Peter (2003) *The Secret State: Whitehall and the Cold War*, London: Penguin Books.

Howell, Sabrina T., Jason Rathje, John Van Reenen and Jun Wong (2021) Opening up military innovation: causal effects of 'bottom-up' reforms to U.S. defense research, NBER Working Paper 28700, April.

Kalnins, Arturs and Kyel J. Mayer (2004) Relationships and hybrid contracts: an analysis of contract choice in information technology, *The Journal of Law, Economics and Organisation*, 20(1), 207–29.

Kapstein, Ethan B. and Jean-Michel Oudot (2009) Reforming defense procurement: lessons from France, *Business and Politics*, 11(2), 1–25.

Kincaid, Bill (2008) *Changing the Dinosaur's Spots: The Battle to Reform UK Defence Acquisition*, London: RUSI Books.

Kirkpatrick, David L. I. (1996) *Choose Your Weapon, Combined Operational Effectiveness and Investment Appraisal (COEIA) and Its Role in UK Defence Procurement*, Whitehall Papers 36, Royal United Services Institute.

Kirkpatrick, David L. I. (2004) Trends in the costs of weapons systems and the consequences, *Defence and Peace Economics*, 15(3), 259–74.

Kirkpatrick, David (2019) The whole-life costs of defence equipment, chapter 13 of Matthews (2019a), 284–306.

Kirkpatrick, David (2021) *How Important Are Superior Numbers?* Cambridge Elements: Defence Economics, Cambridge, UK: Cambridge University Press.

Kolodziej, Edward, A. (1987) *Making and Marketing Arms: The French Experience and Its Implications for the International System*, Princeton, NJ: Princeton University Press.

Levene, Peter (2011) *Defence Reform: An Independent Report into the Structure and Management of the Ministry of Defence*, London: The Stationery Office.

Luttwak, Edward N. (1985) *The Pentagon and the Art of War*, New York: Simon and Schuster.

Magill, Peter (2021) Collaborative defence procurement in a post-Brexit world: the Anglo-French case, *The RUSI Journal*, 166(2), 62–70.

Matthews, Ron, editor (2019a) *The Political Economy of Defence*, Cambridge, UK: Cambridge University Press.

Matthews, Ron (2019b) The rise and demise of government-mandated offset policy, chapter 7 of Matthews (2019a), 148–68.

Matthews, Ron and Rashid Al-Saadi (2021) Organisational complexity of the Eurofighter Typhoon collaborative supply chain, *Defence and Peace Economics*, http://doi.org/10.1080/10242694.2021.1987022.

Mazzucato, Mariana (2013) *The Entrepreneurial State: Debunking Public vs Private Sector Myths*, London: Anthem Press.

Moretti, Enrico, Claudia Steinwender and John Van Reenen (2021) The intellectual spoils of war? Defense R&D, productivity and international spillovers, Centre for Economic Performance Discussion Paper 1662.

NAO (1993) *Accounting for Inflation in Defence Procurement*. London: National Audit Office.

NAO (2020a) *Managing Infrastructure Projects on Nuclear-Regulated Sites*, London: National Audit Office, HC 19, Session 2019–20.

NAO (2020b) *Defence Capabilities – Delivering What Was Promised*, London: National Audit Office, HC 106, Session 2019–21.

NAO (2021) *Improving the Performance of Major Equipment Contracts*, London: National Audit Office, HC 298, Session 2021–22.

Oudot, Jean-Michel and Renaud Bellais (2019) Defence companies in the age of globalisation: French defence industry as a case study, chapter 8 of Matthews (2019a), 169–94.

PAC (2005) *Ministry of Defence: The Rapid Procurement of Capability to Support Operations*, London: House of Commons Public Accounts Committee.

PAC (2021a) *Report on Equipment Plan*, London: House of Commons Public Accounts Committee.

PAC (2021b) *Improving the Performance of Major Defence Equipment Contracts*, London: House of Commons Public Accounts Committee, HC 185.

Peck, Merton J. and Frederick M. Scherer (1962) *The Weapons Acquisition Process – An Economic Analysis*, Cambridge, MA: Division of Research, Harvard Business School.

RAND Europe (2021) *Persistent Challenges in UK Defence Equipment Acquisition*, Cambridge, UK: RAND Corporation.

Rogerson, William P. (1994) Economic incentives and the defense procurement process, *Journal of Economic Perspectives*, 8(4), 65–90.

Rogerson, William P. (1995) Incentive models of the defense procurement process, chapter 12 of Hartley and Sandler (1995), 309–46.

Ruttan, Vernon W. (2006) *Is War Necessary for Economic Growth? Military Procurement and Technology Development*, Oxford: Oxford University Press.

Sandler, Todd and Keith Hartley (1995) *The Economics of Defense*, Cambridge, UK: Cambridge University Press.

Scherer, Frederick M. (1964) *The Weapons Acquisition Process: Economic Incentives*, Cambridge, MA: Harvard University Press.

SIPRI (2021) *The SIPRI Yearbook: Armaments, Disarmament and International Security*, Stockholm International Peace Research Institute, Oxford: Oxford University Press.

Smith, Ron P. (2009) *Military Economics, the Interaction of Power and Money*, Basingstoke: Palgrave.

Spenkuch, Jorg L., Edoardo Teso and Guo Xu (2021) Ideology and performance in public organizations, NBER Working Paper No. 28673.

Taylor, Trevor (2019) Defence procurement: overcoming challenges and managing expectations, chapter 12 of Matthews (2019a), 258–83.

Taylor, Trevor (2022) Lessons from the Ajax programme, Emerging Insights, Royal United Services Institute, January 2022.

Uttley, Matt and Benedict Wilkinson (2019) The great paradox of defence: political economy and defence procurement in post-Brexit United Kingdom, chapter 9 of Matthews (2019a), 195–216.

Warren, Patrick L. (2014) Contracting officer workload, incomplete contracting, and contractual terms, *RAND Journal of Economics*, 45(2), 395–421.

Watters, Bryan (2019) Political versus military leadership: the battle for common means and ends, chapter 2 of Matthews (2019a), 27–46.

Yu, Tinghua (2021) Accountability and learning with motivated agents, *Journal of Theoretical Politics*, 34(2), 313–29.

Acknowledgements

I am grateful to Viv Brown, George Georgiou, Keith Hartley, Ian Holder and David Kirkpatrick for very useful comments on earlier versions, but all errors and opinions are mine.

Cambridge Elements ☰

Defence Economics

Keith Hartley
University of York

Keith Hartley was Professor of Economics and Director of the Centre for Defence Economics at the University of York, where he is now Emeritus Professor of Economics. He is the author of over 500 publications comprising journal articles, books and reports. His most recent books include *The Economics of Arms* (Agenda Publishing, 2017) and with Jean Belin (eds.) *The Economics of the Global Defence Industry* (Taylor and Francis, 2020). Hartley was founding editor of the journal *Defence and Peace Economics*; a NATO Research Fellow; a QinetiQ Visiting Fellow; consultant to the UN, EC, EDA, UK MoD, HM Treasury, Trade and Industry, Business, Innovation and Skills and International Development and previously Special Adviser to the House of Commons Defence Committee.

About the Series

Defence Economics is a relatively new field within the discipline of economics. It studies all aspects of the economics of war and peace. It embraces a wide range of topics in both macroeconomics and microeconomics. Cambridge Elements in Defence Economics aims to publish original and authoritative papers in the field. These will include expert surveys of the foundations of the discipline, its historical development and contributions developing new and novel topics. They will be valuable contributions to both research and teaching in universities and colleges, and will also appeal to other specialist groups comprising politicians, military and industrial personnel as well as informed general readers.

Cambridge Elements $\equiv$

Defence Economics

Printed in the United States
by Baker & Taylor Publisher Services